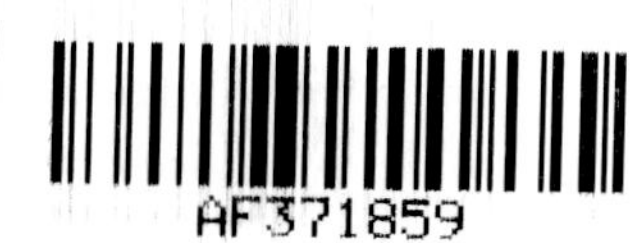

RÉVEILLER LES
MORTS

Adult Edition Zombies Livre a Colorier

Coloring Bandit

Publié par Speedy Publishing Canada Limited

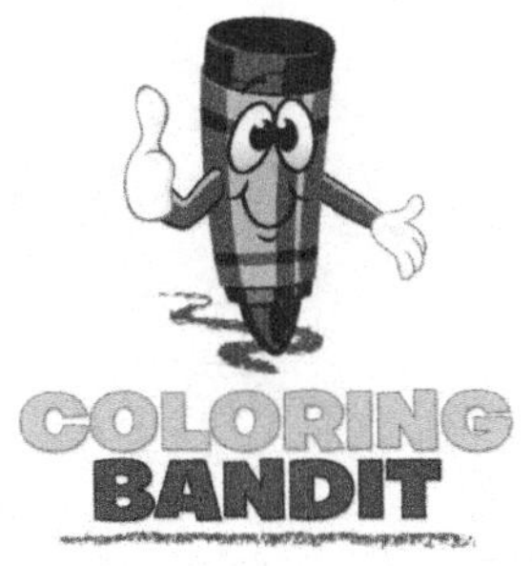

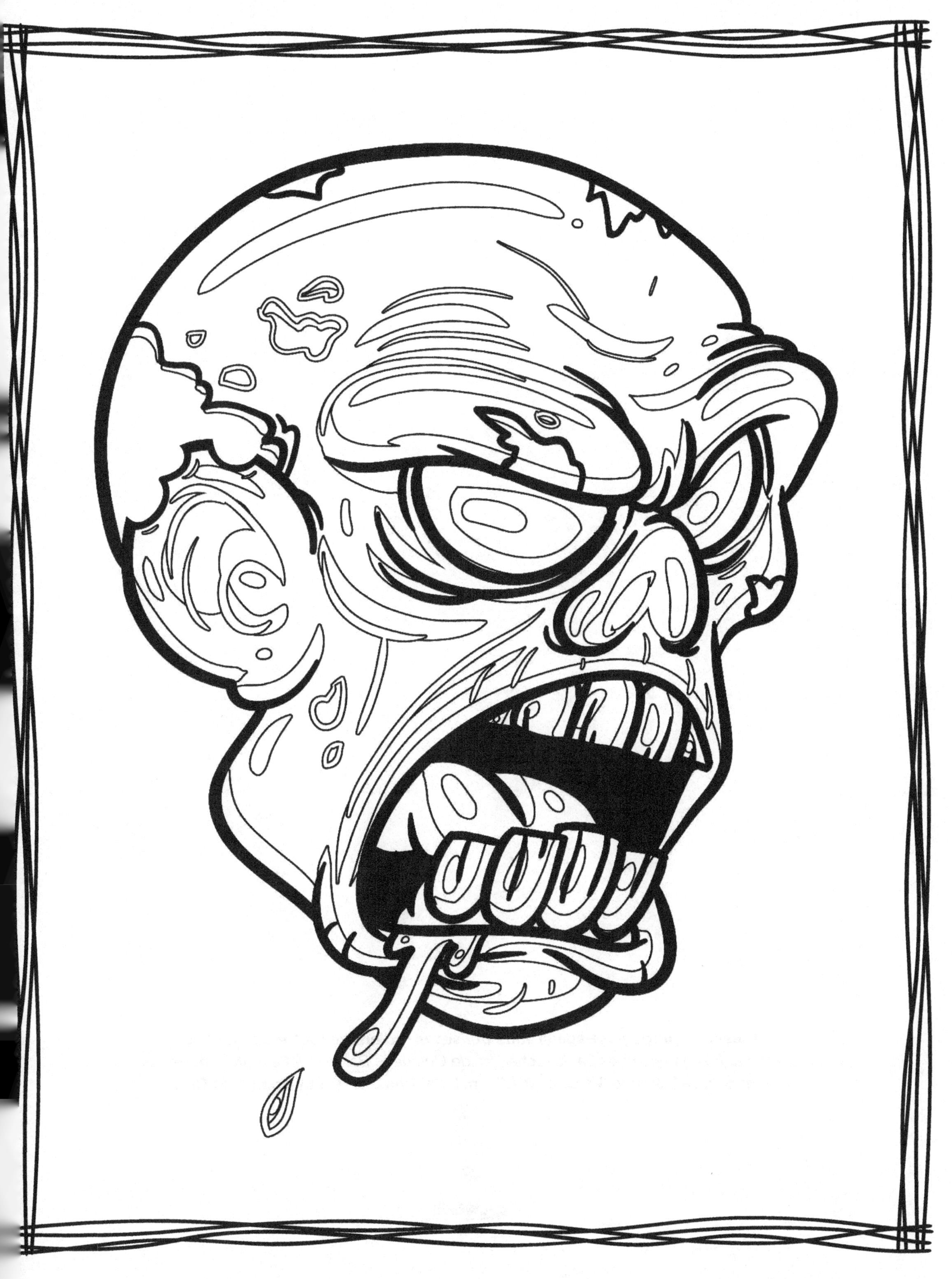

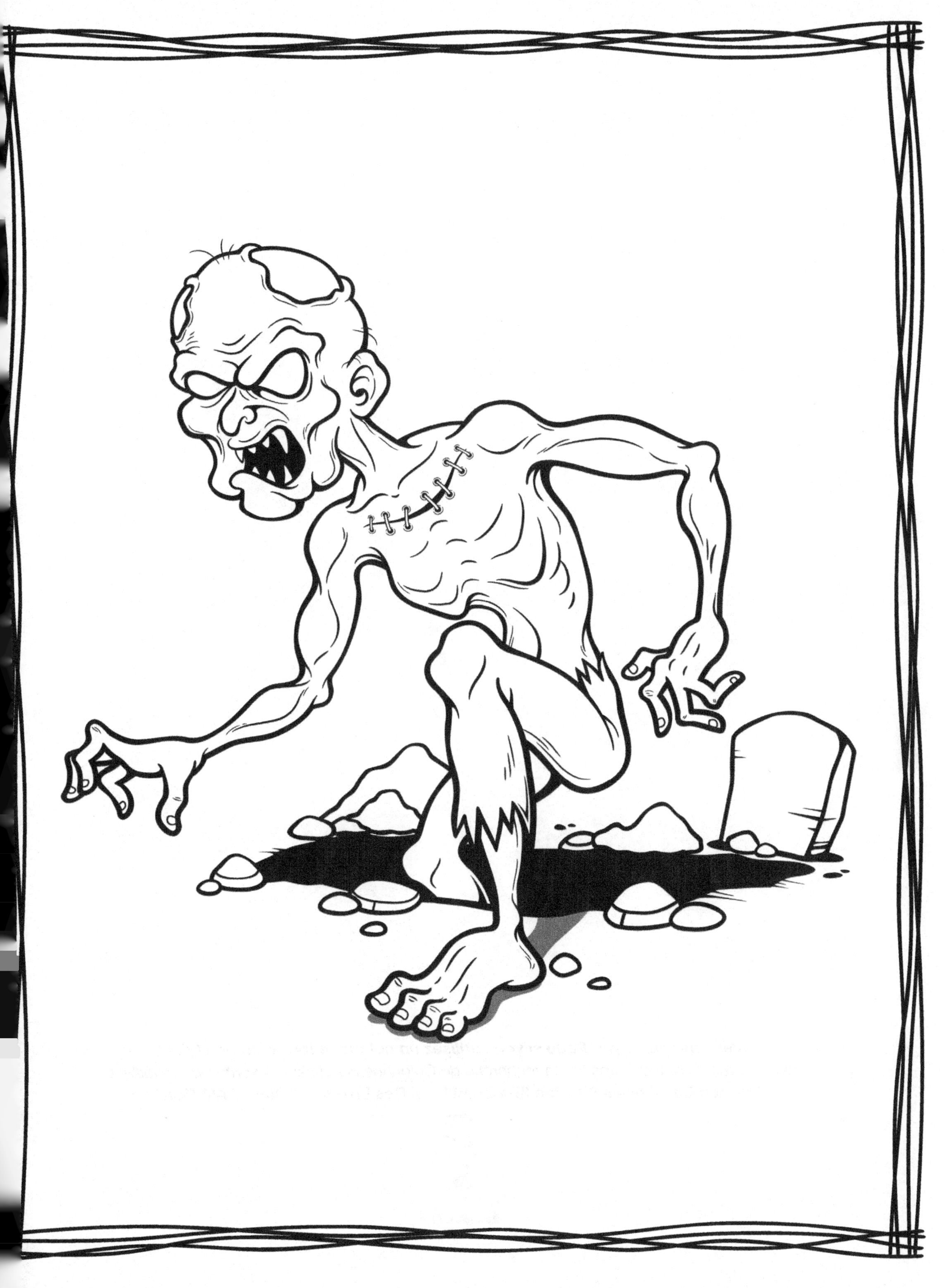

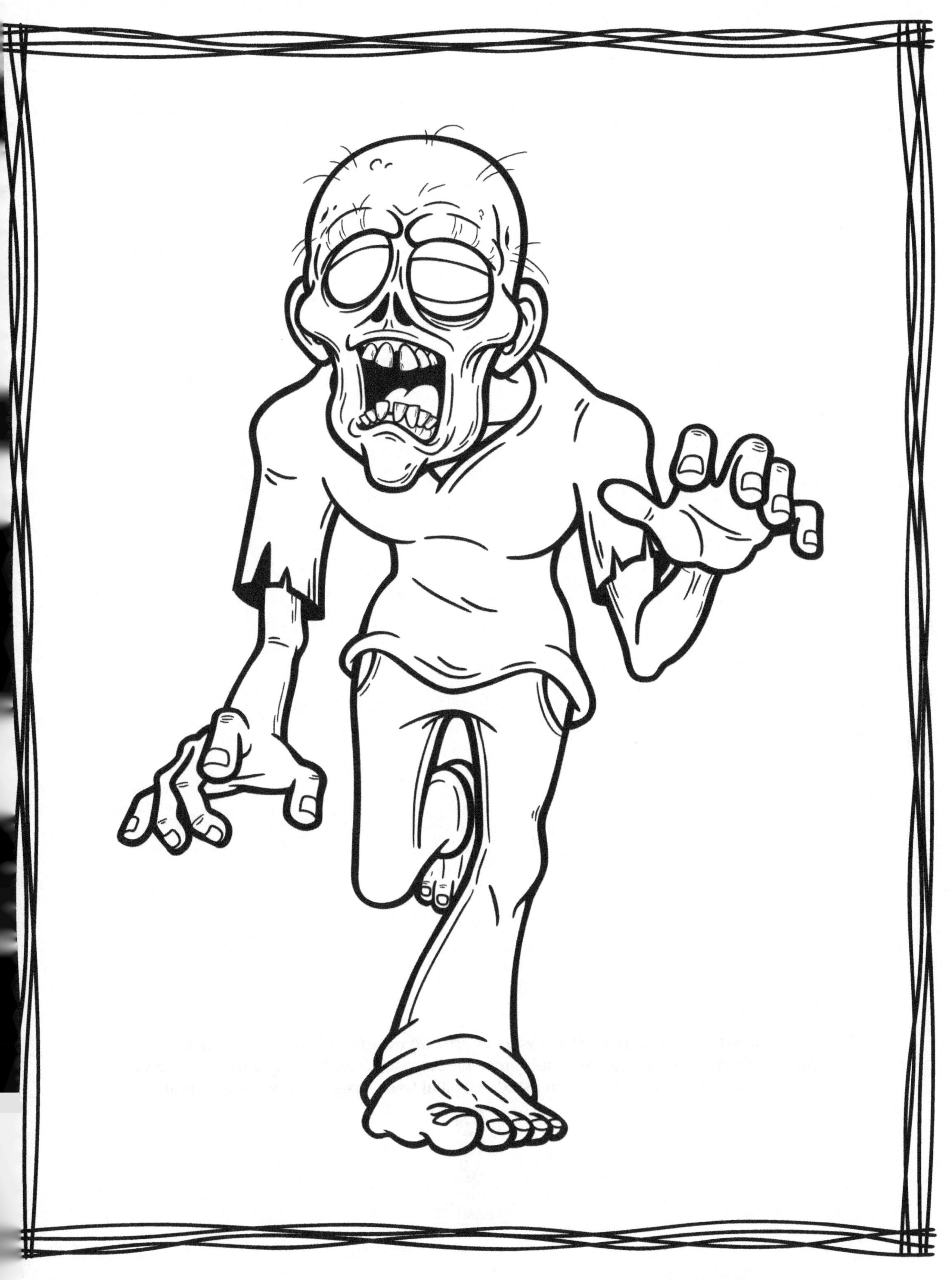

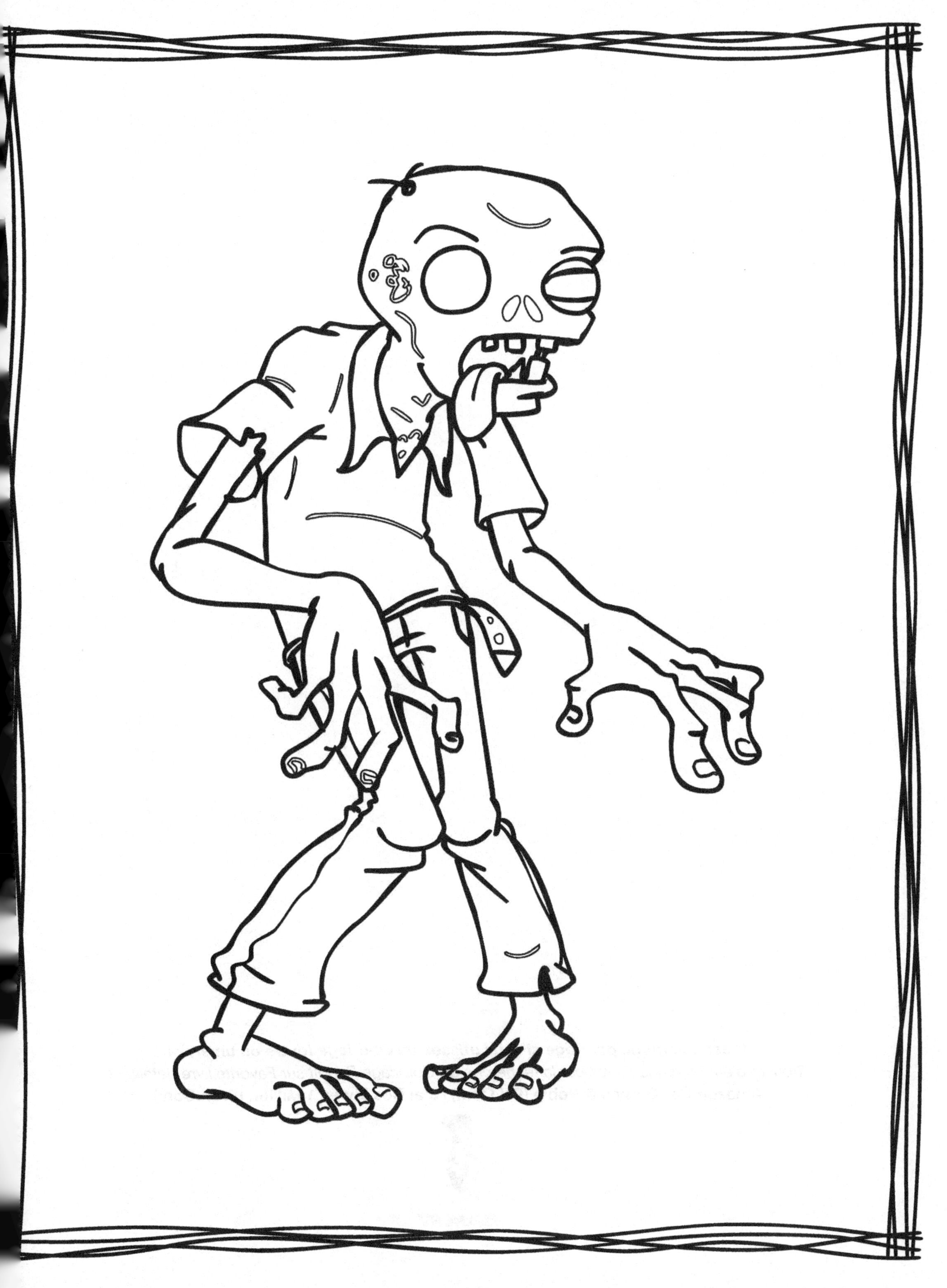

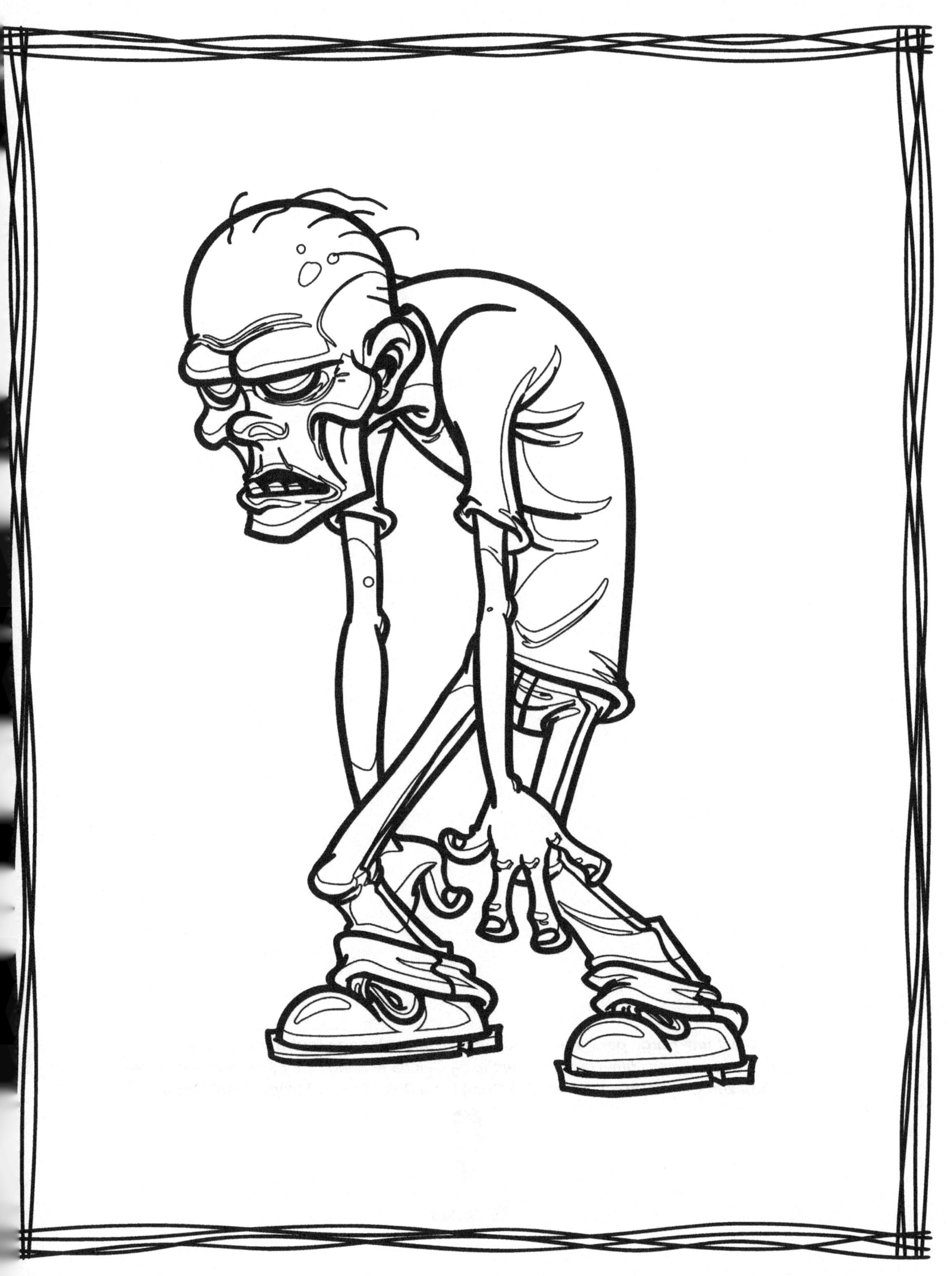

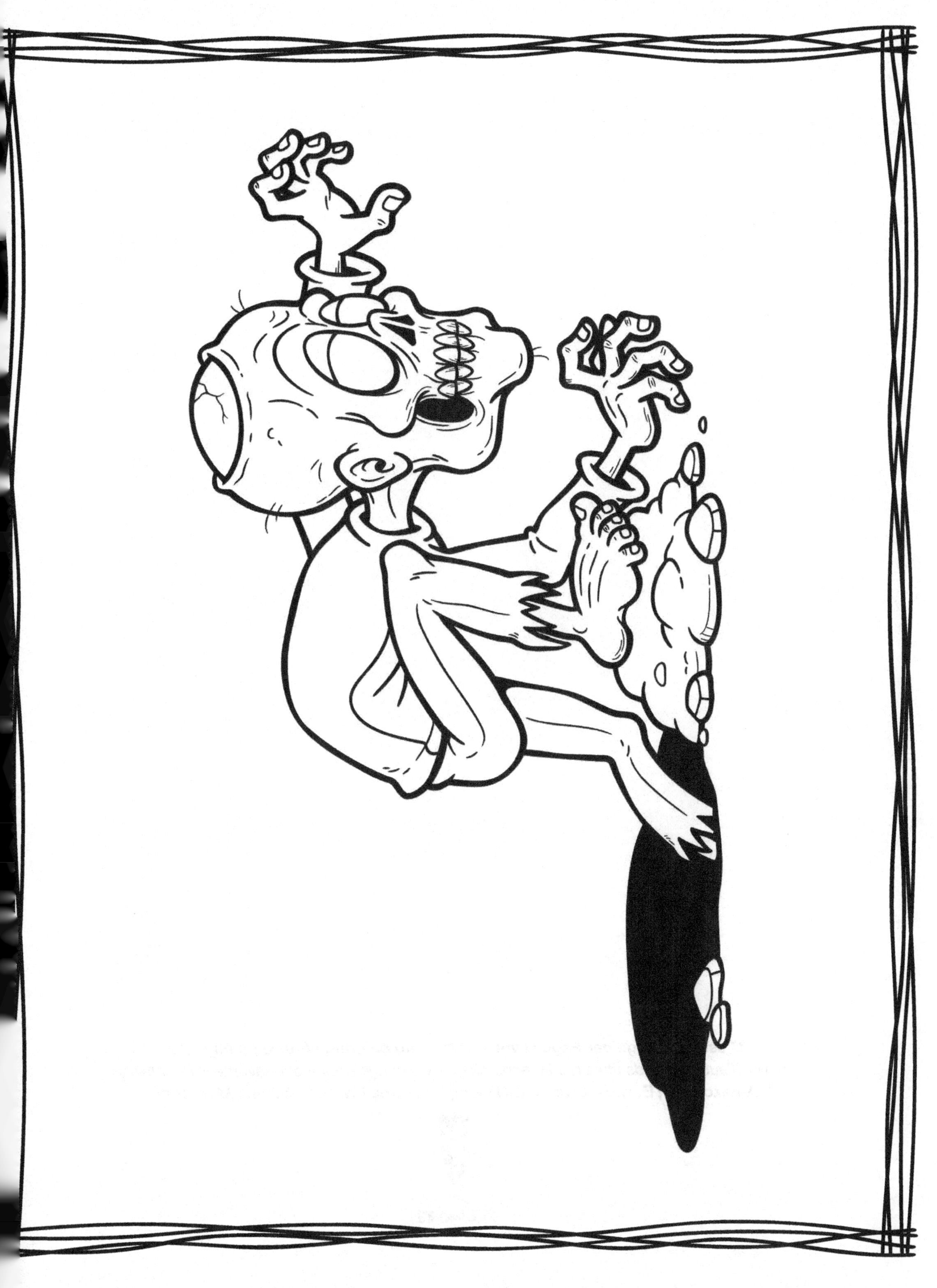

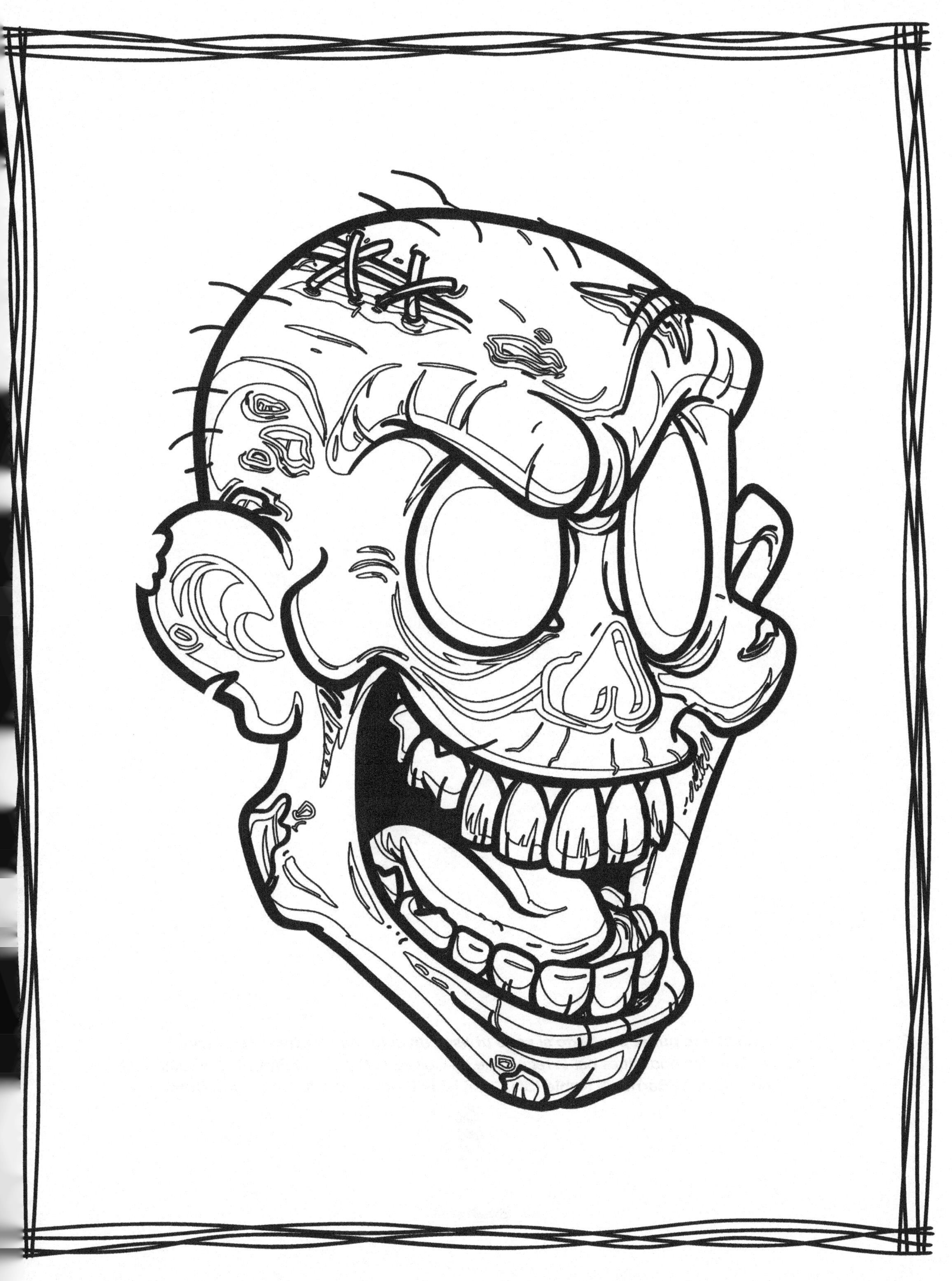

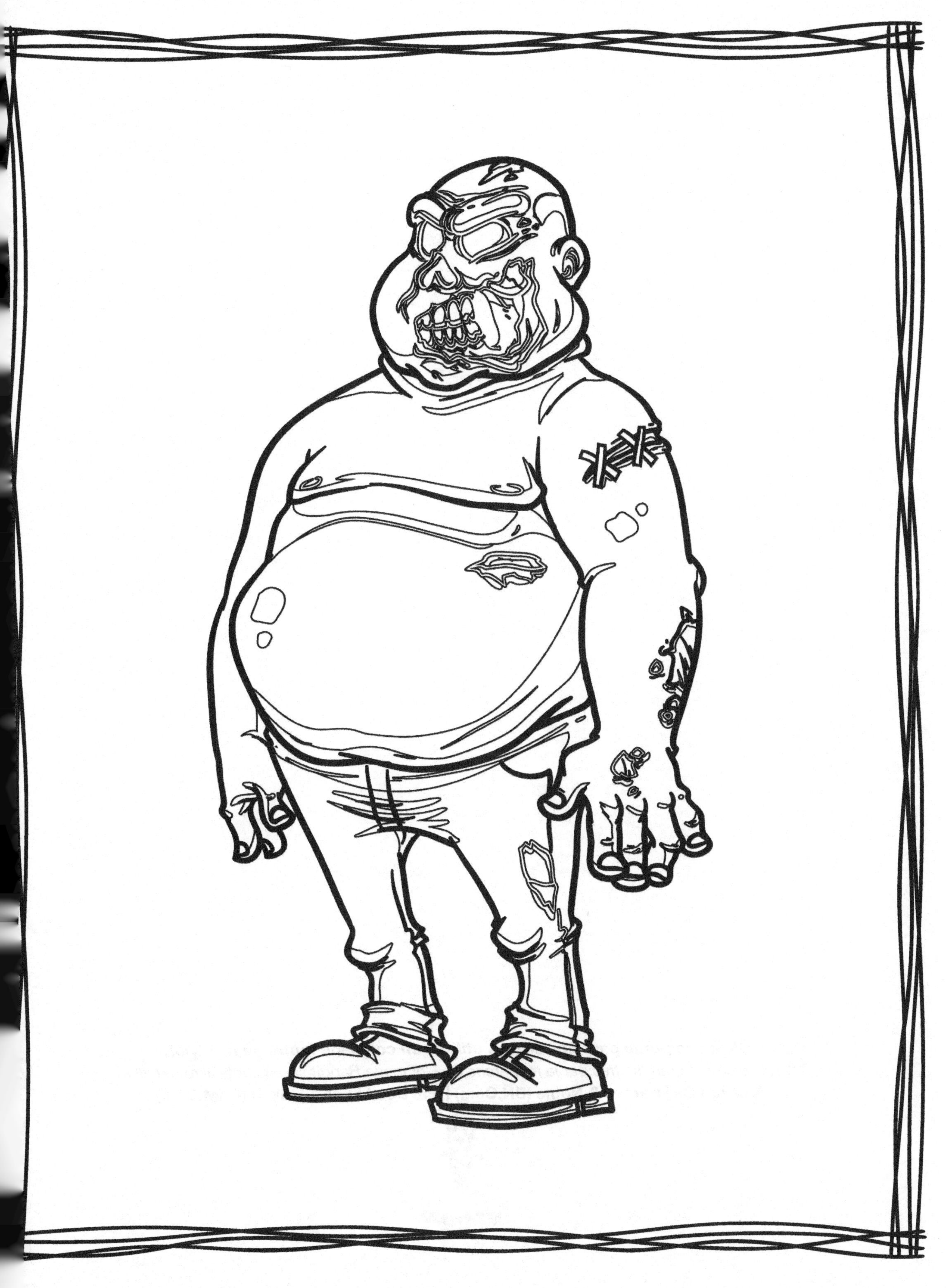

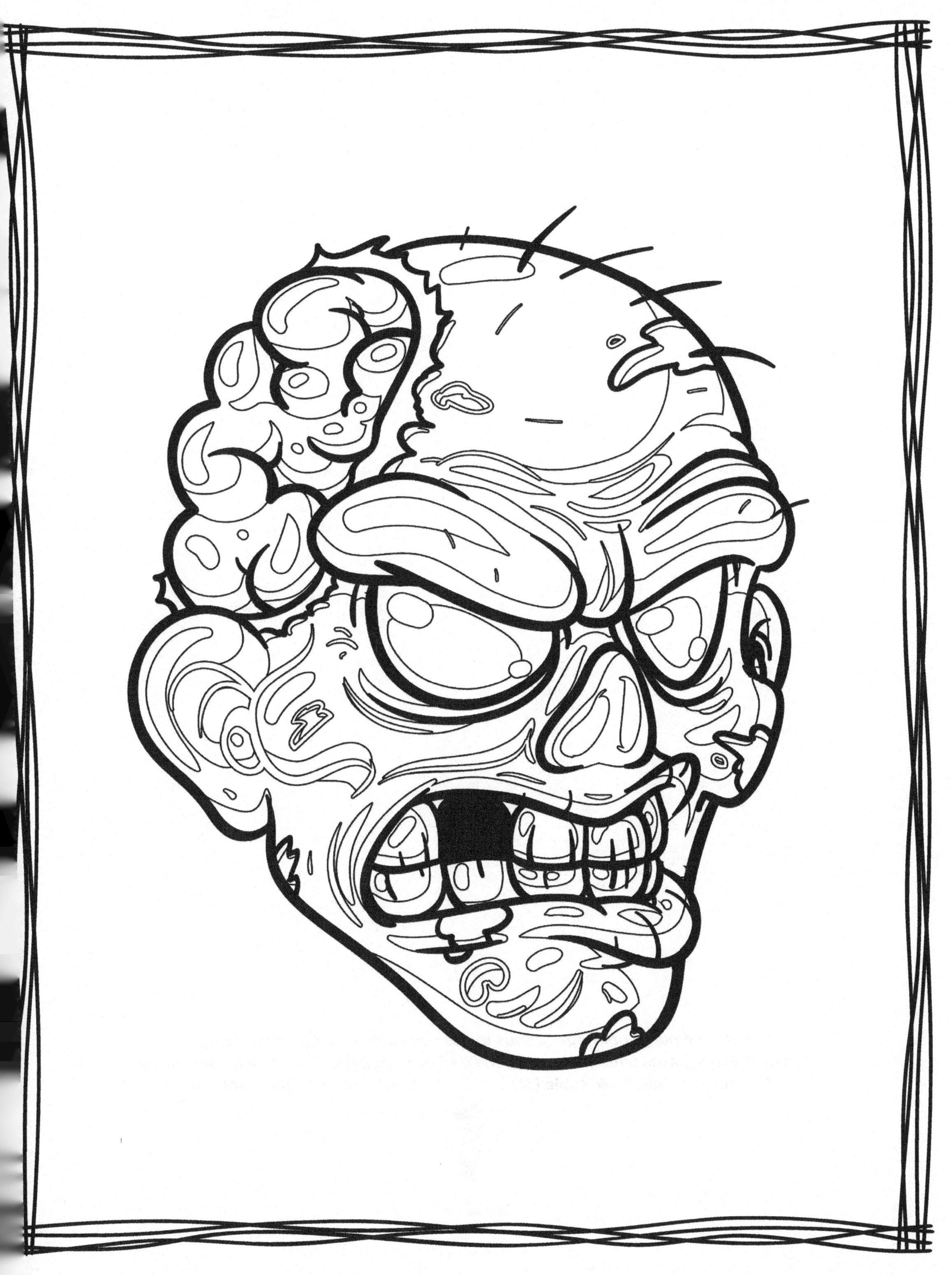

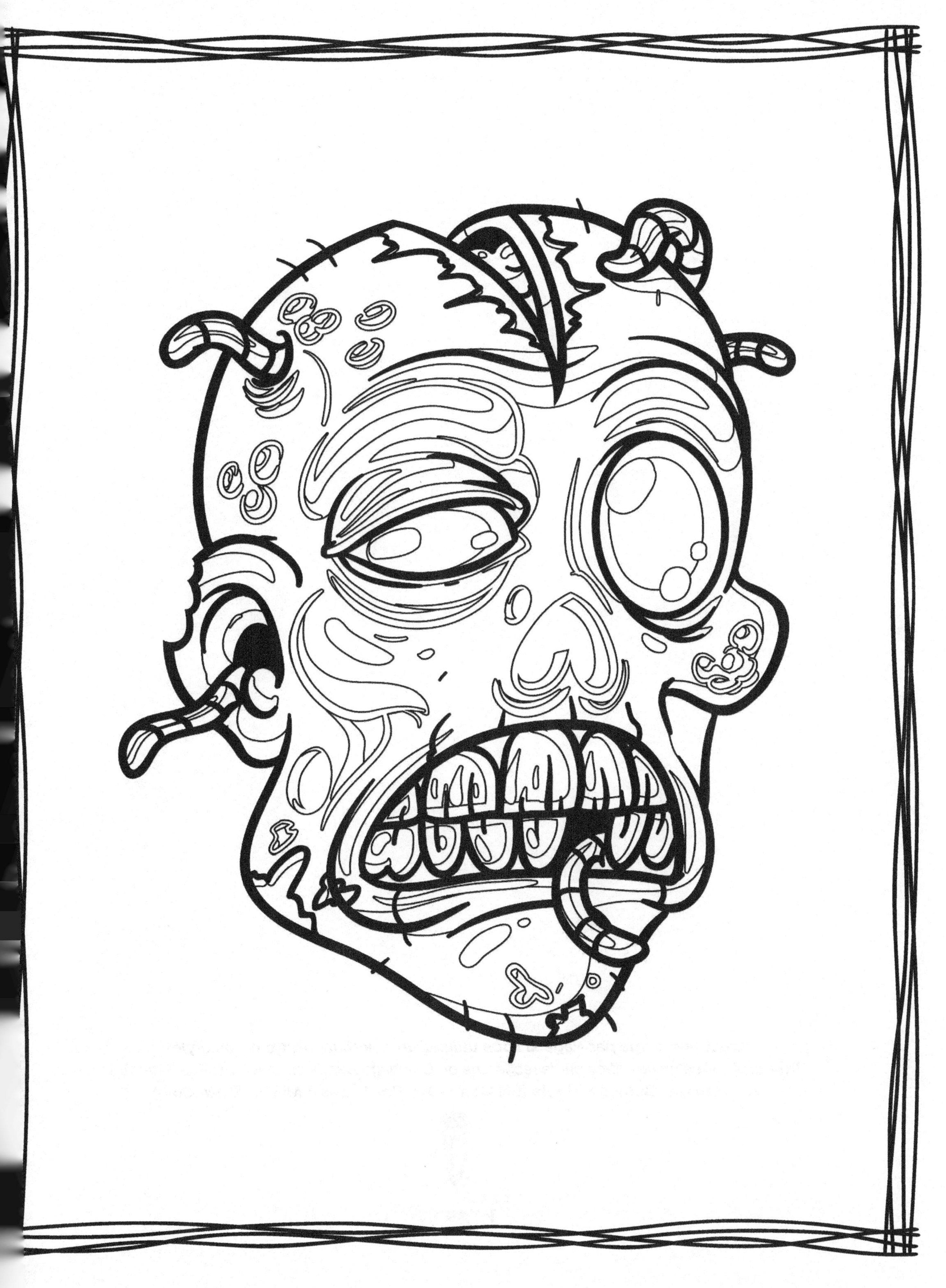

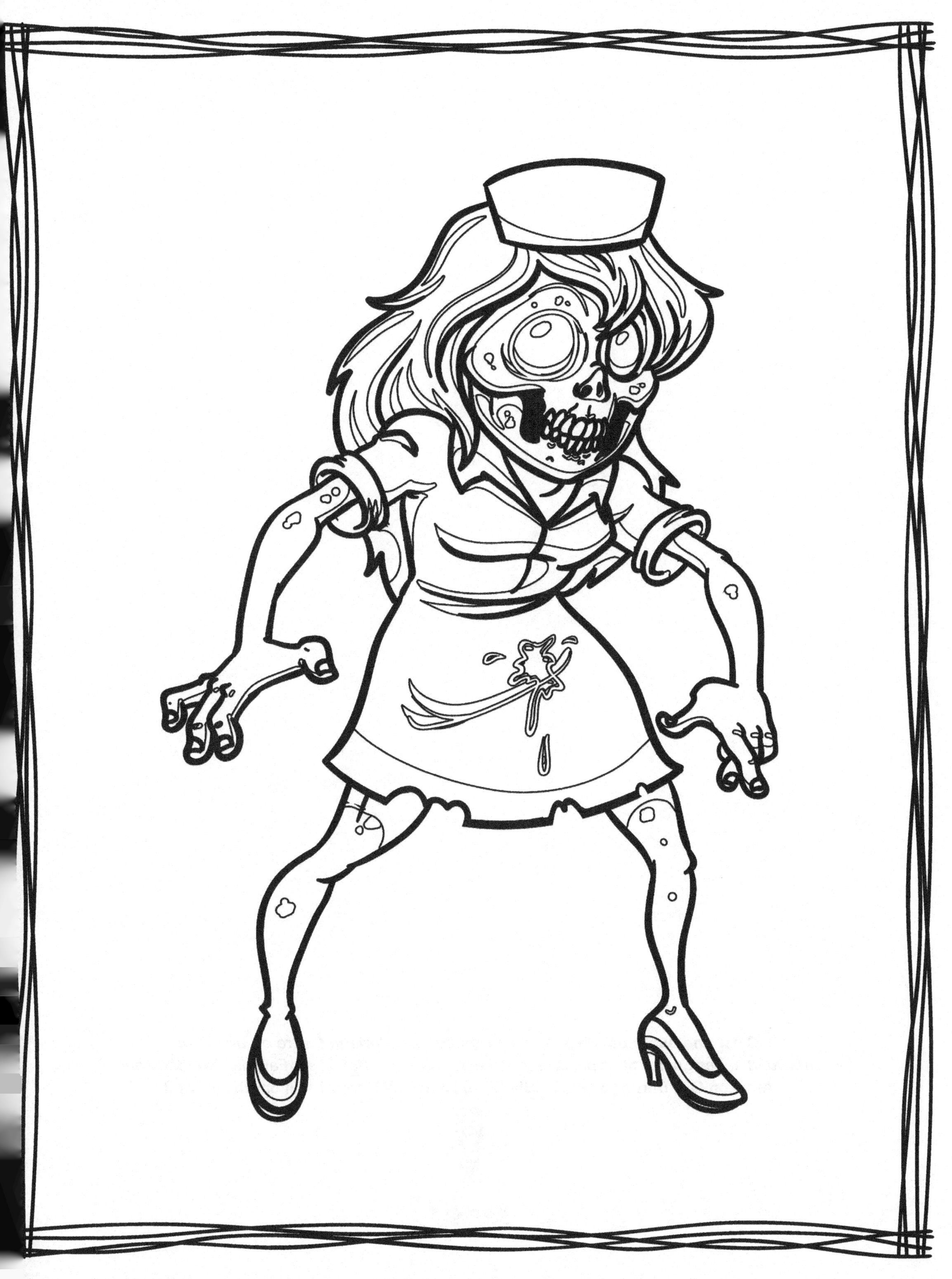

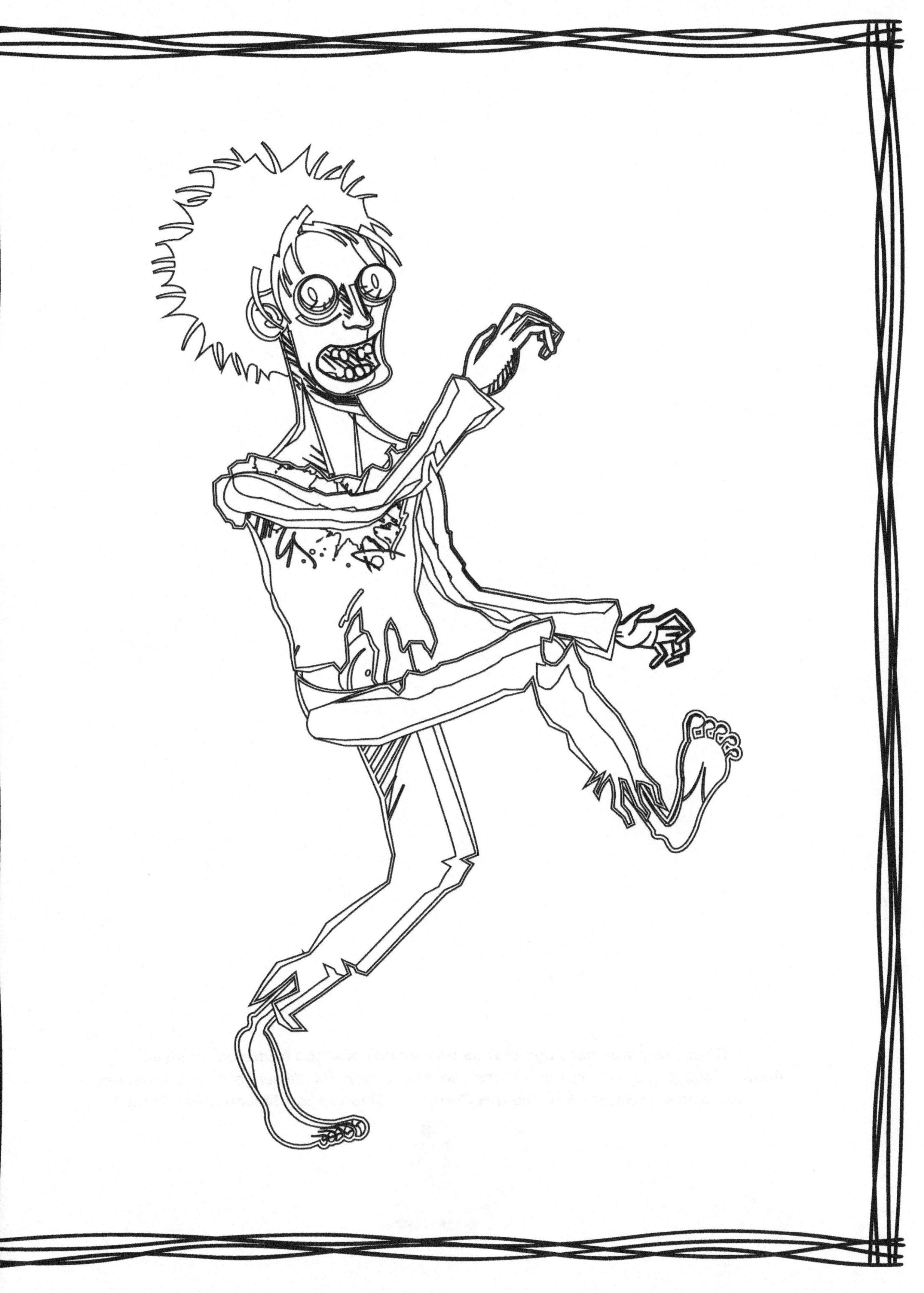

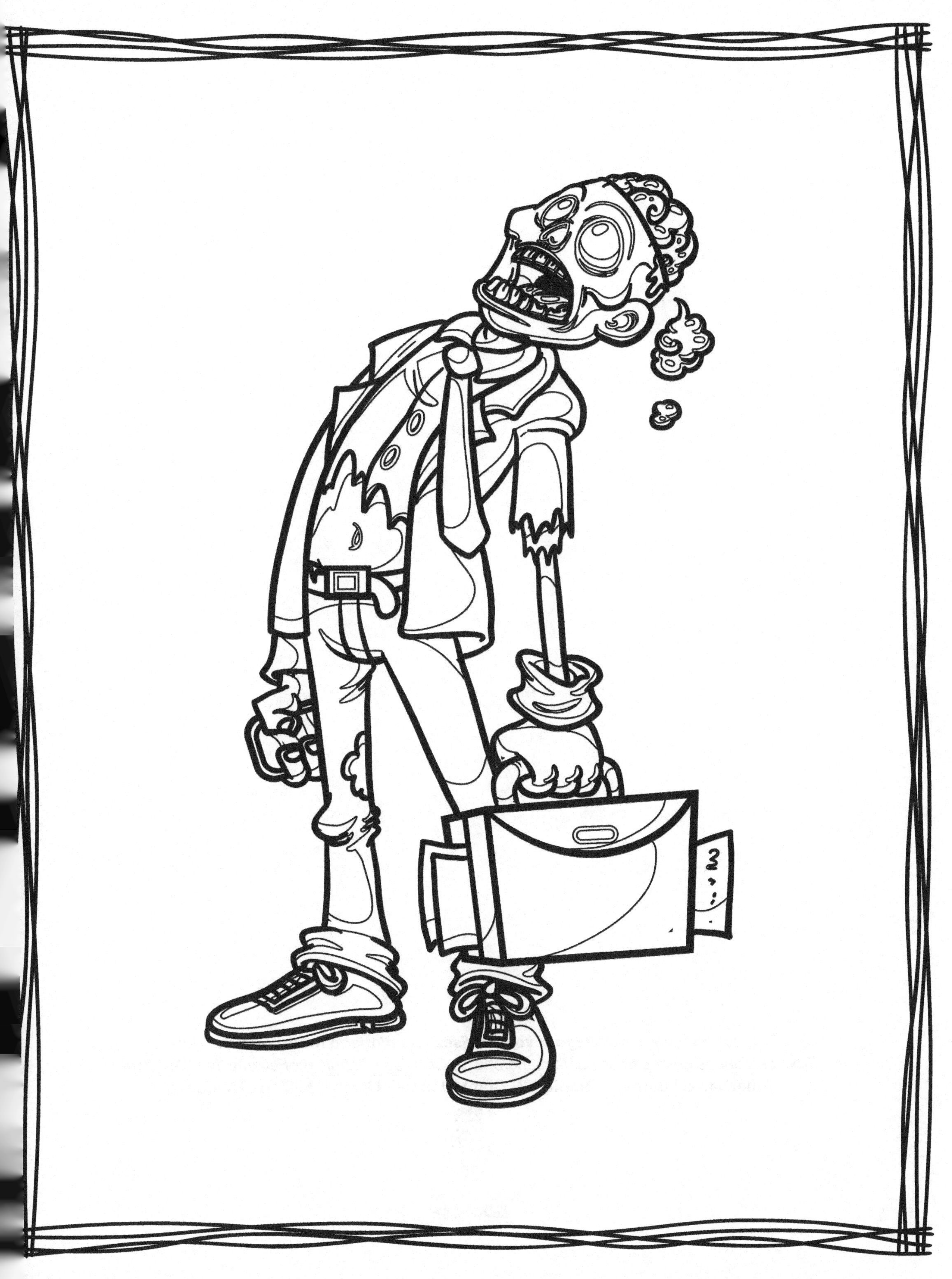

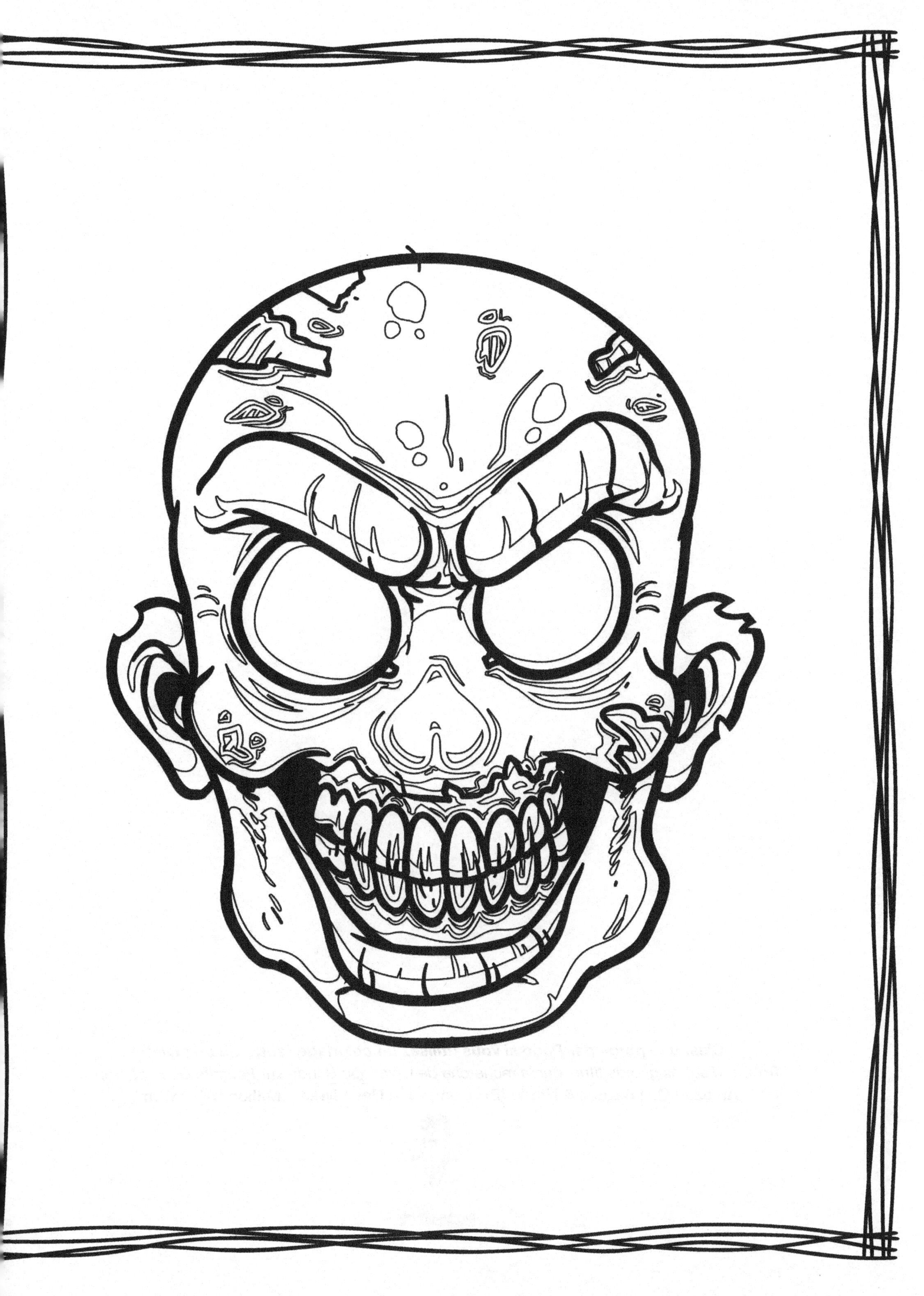

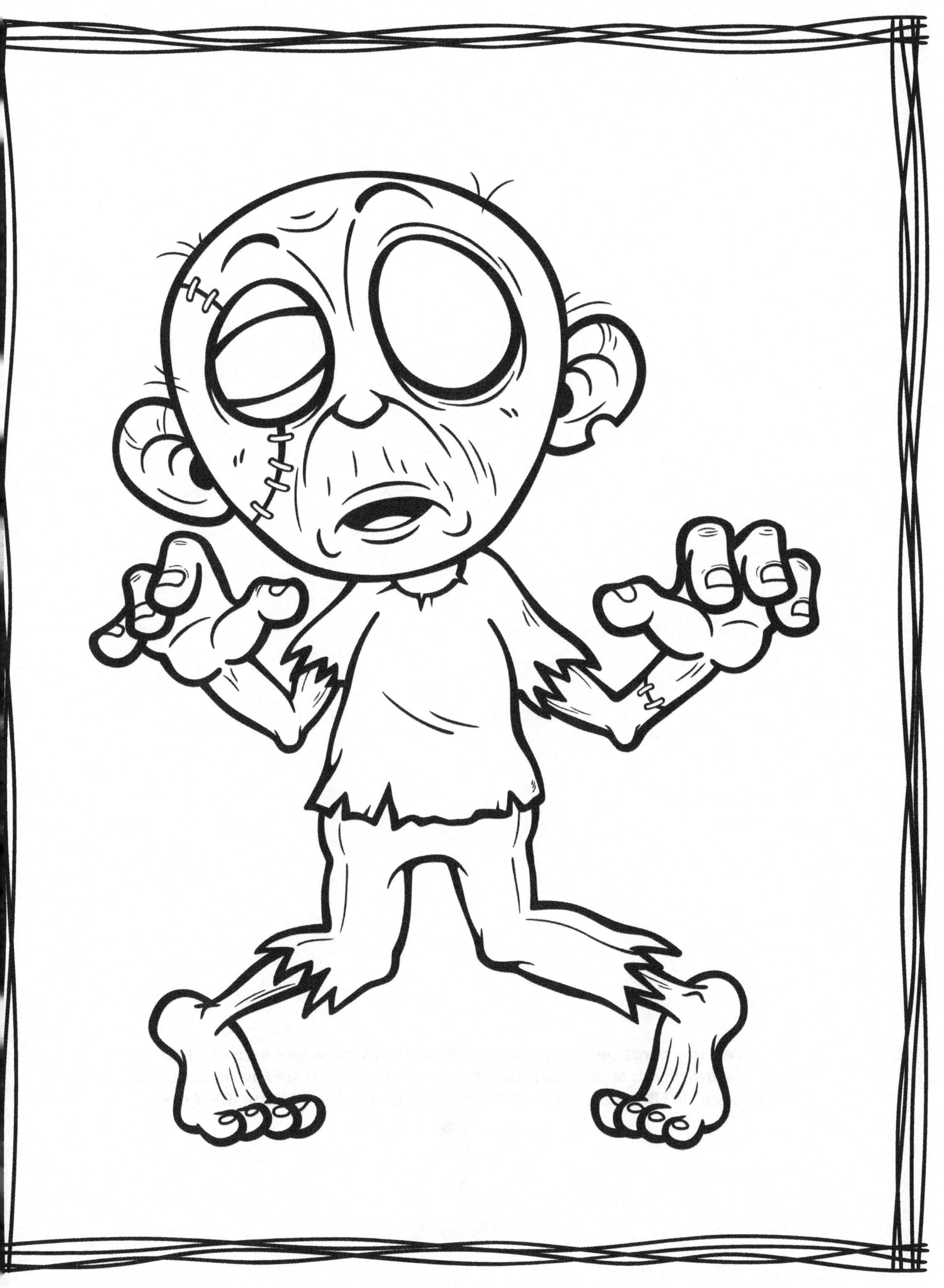

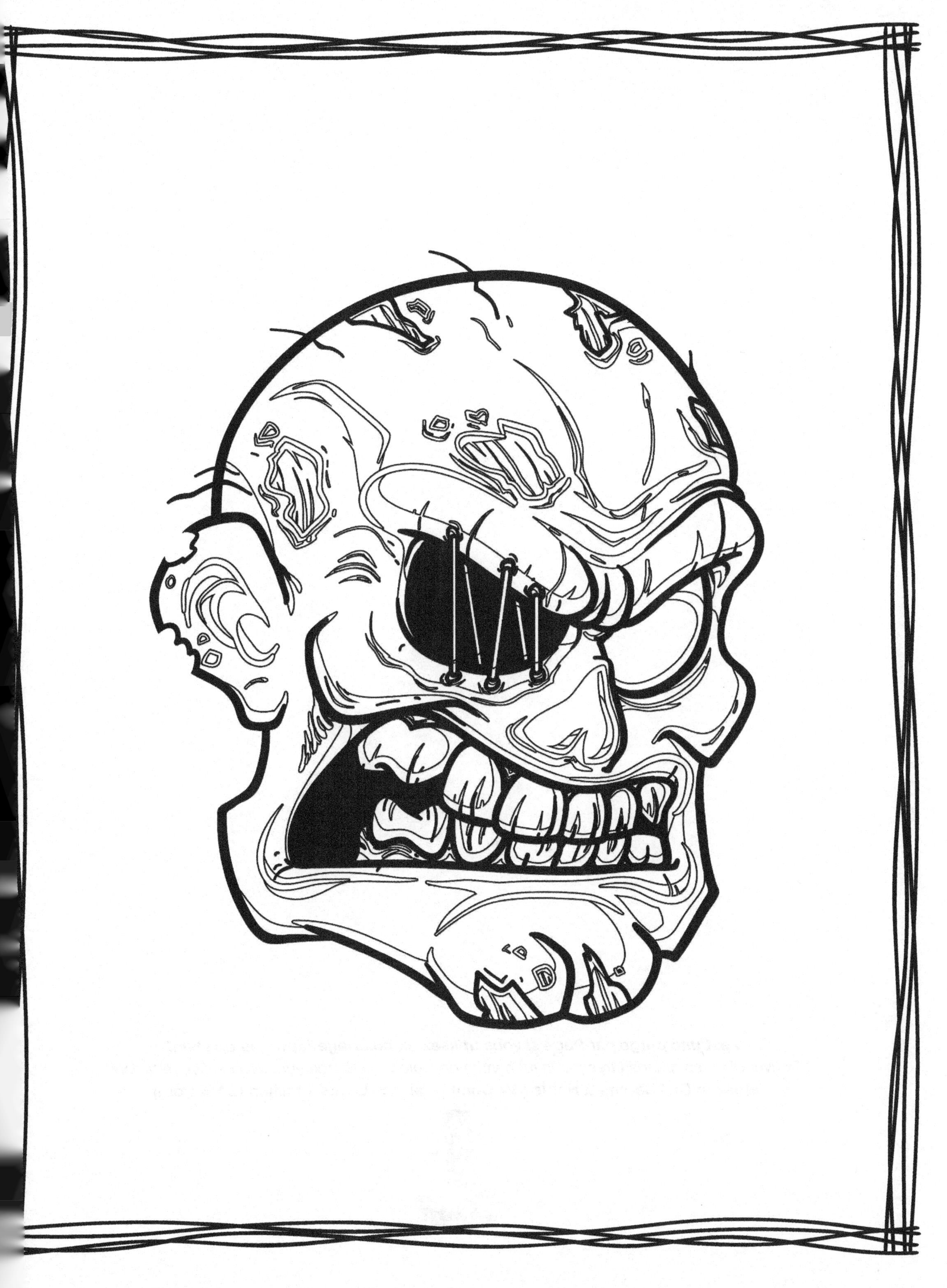

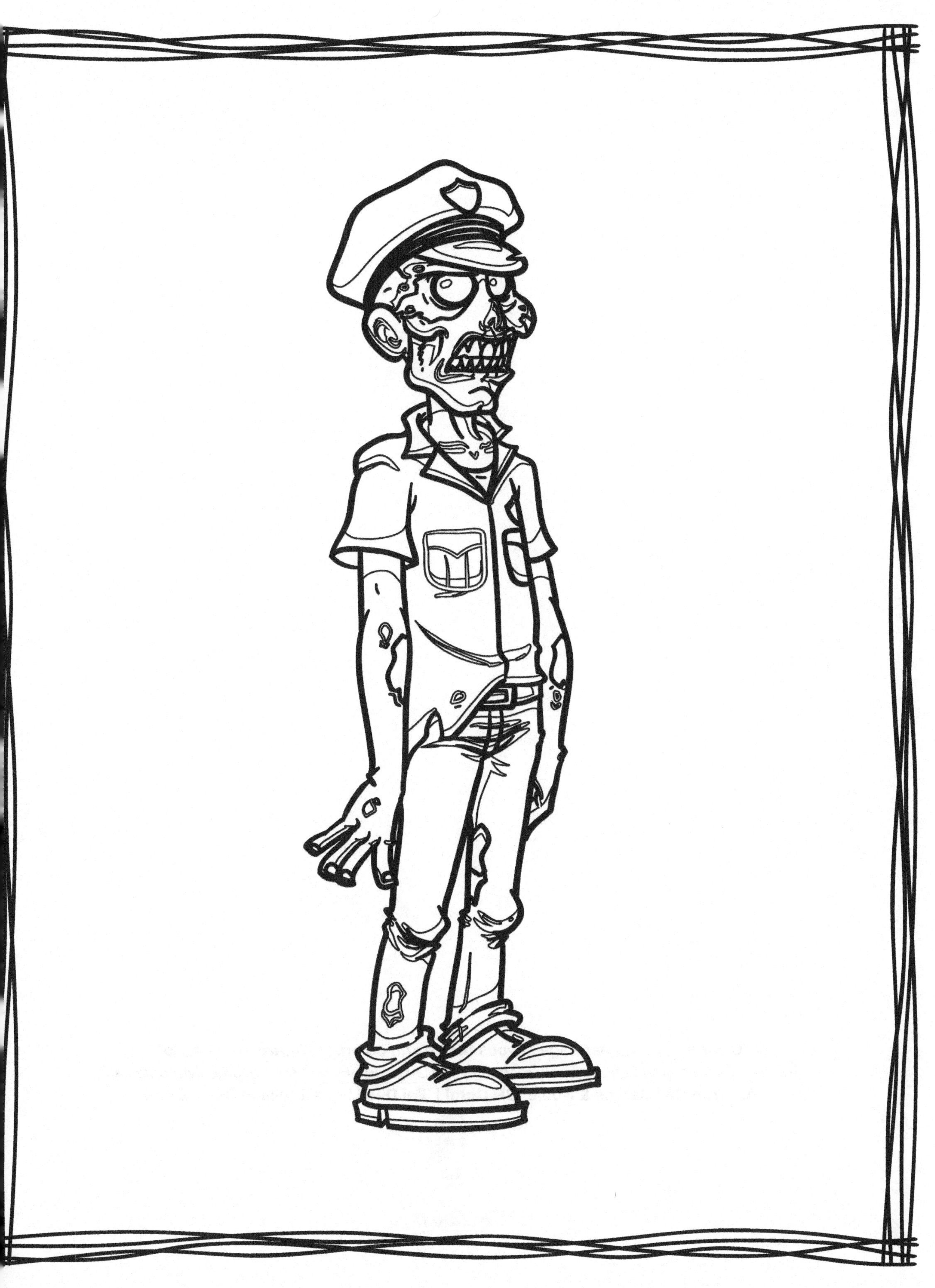

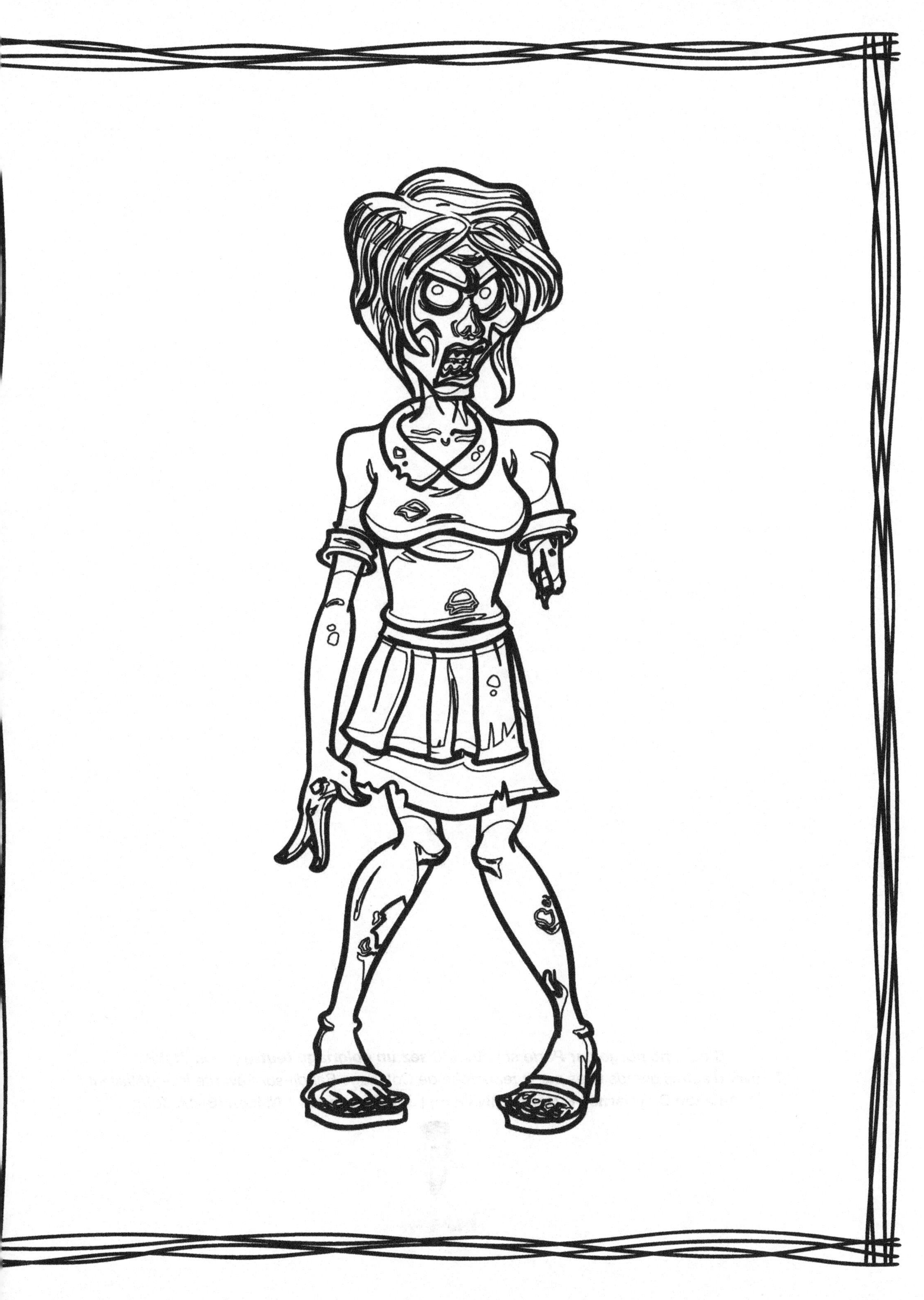

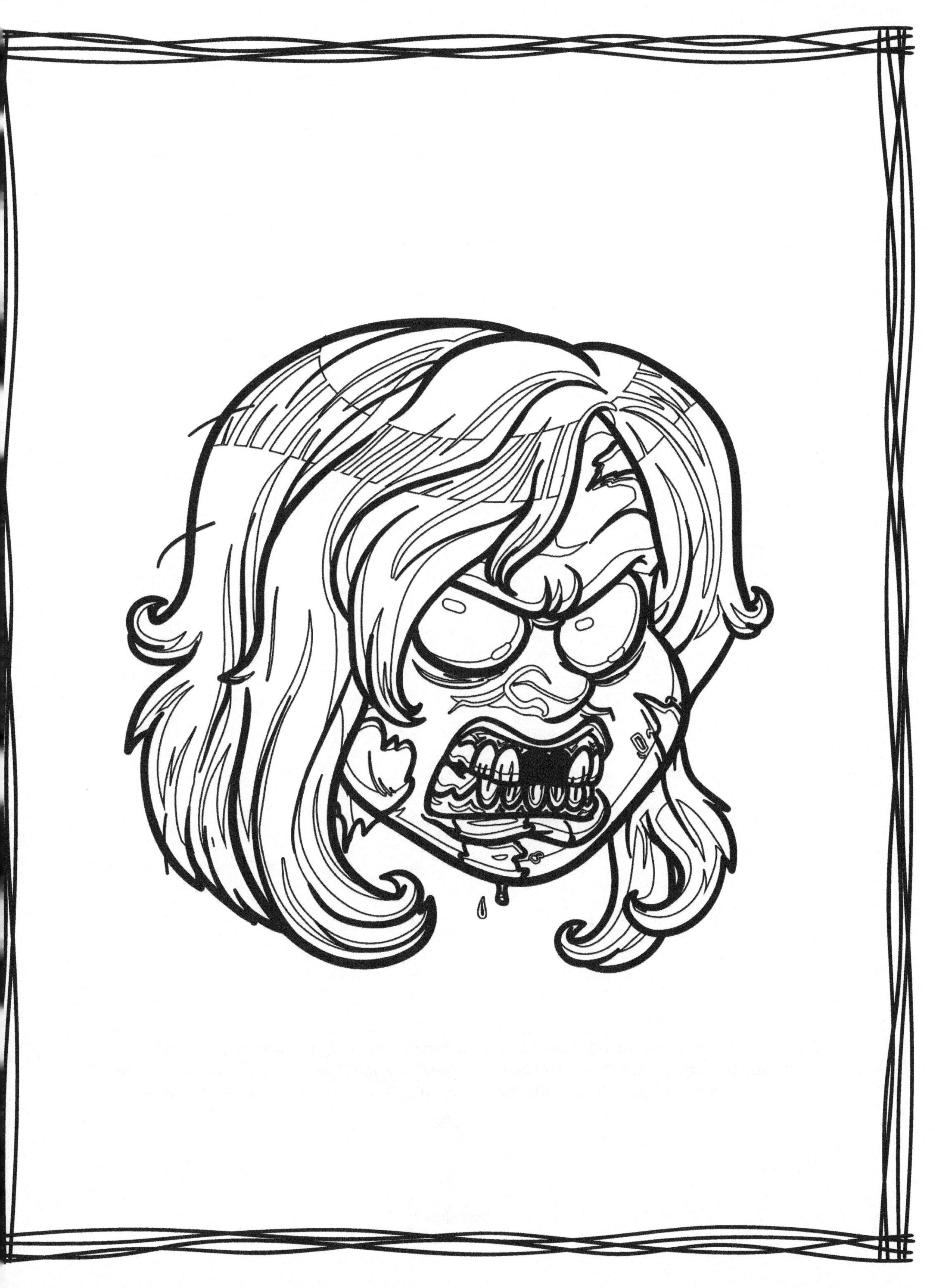

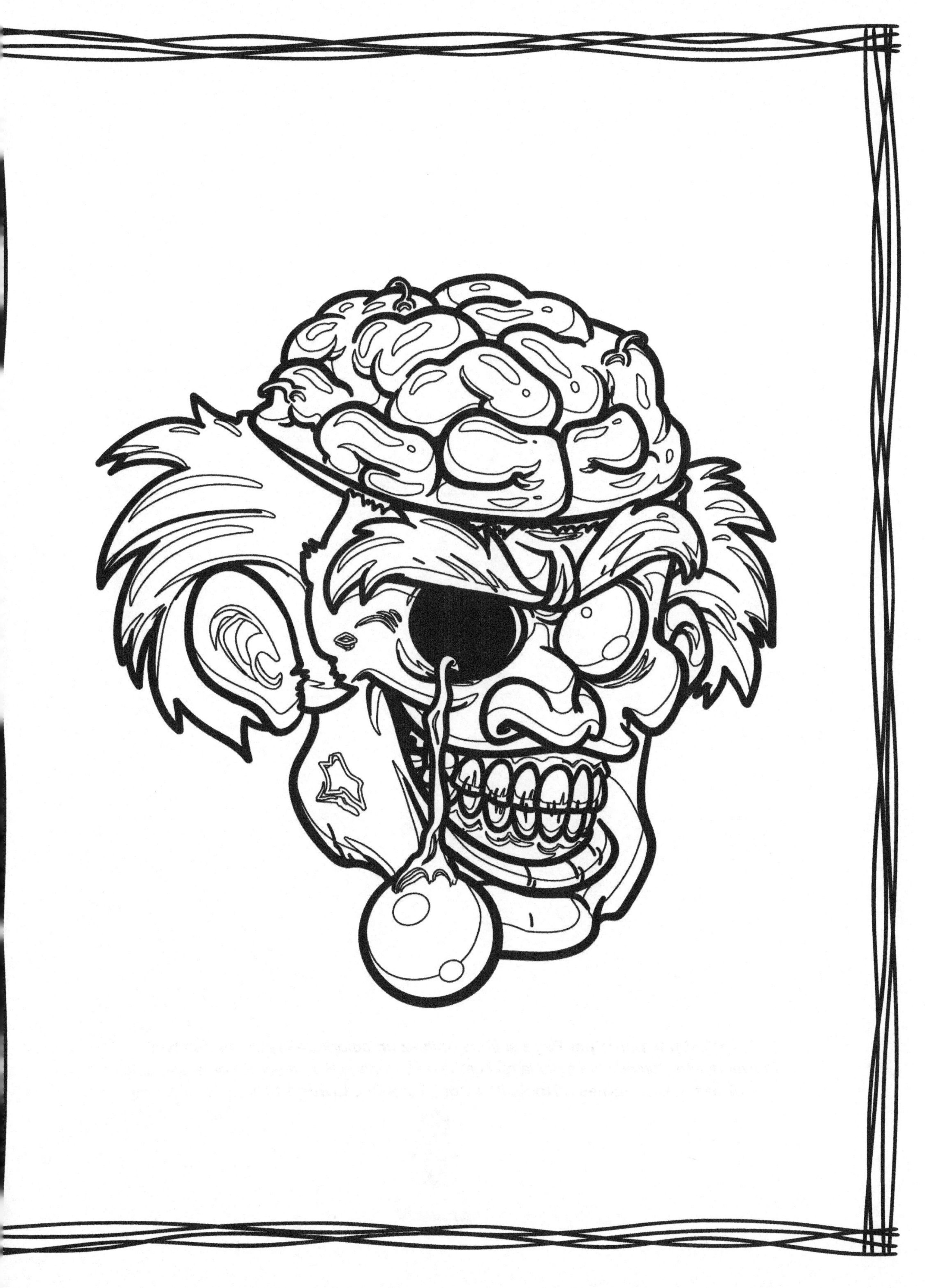

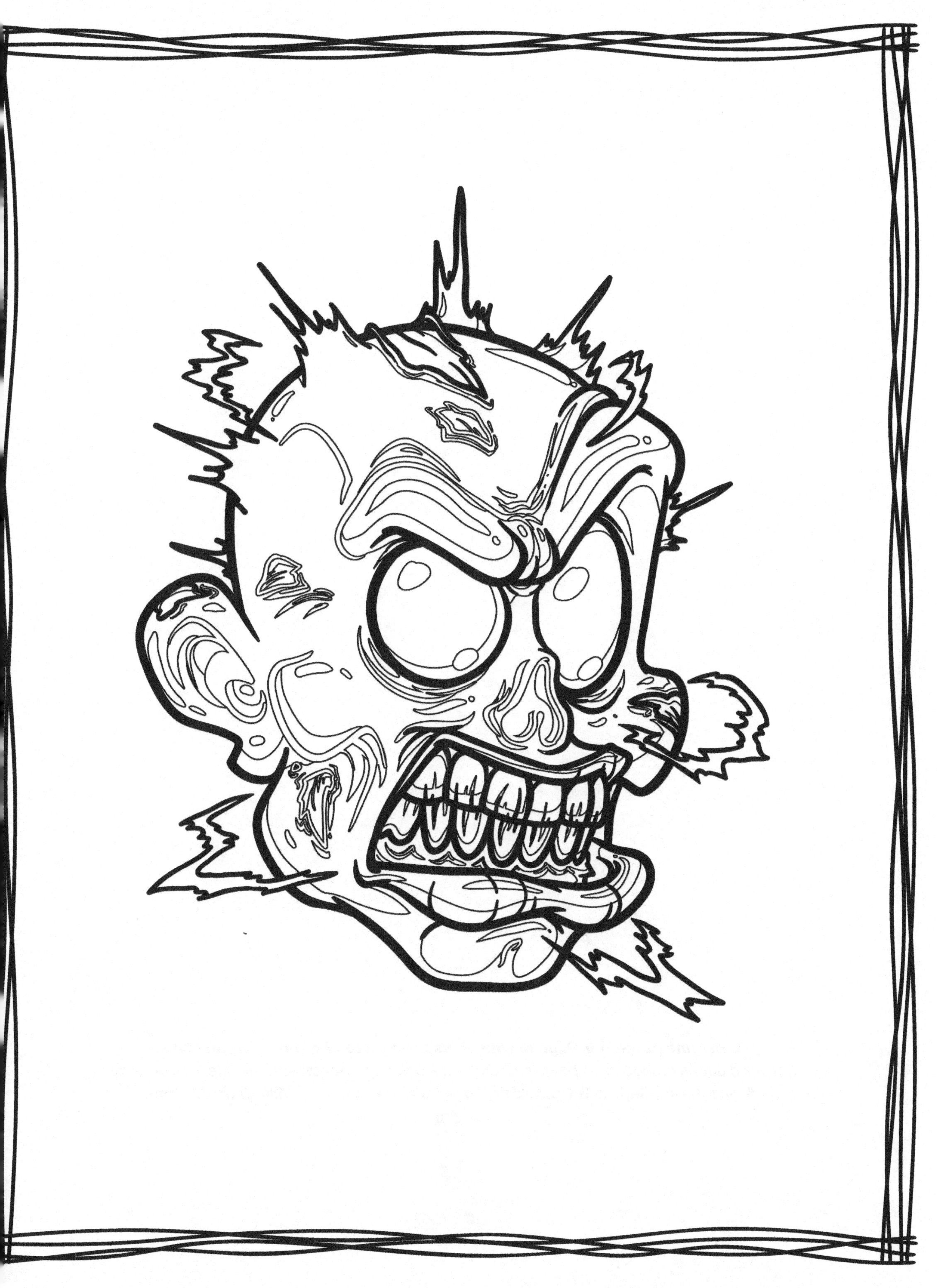

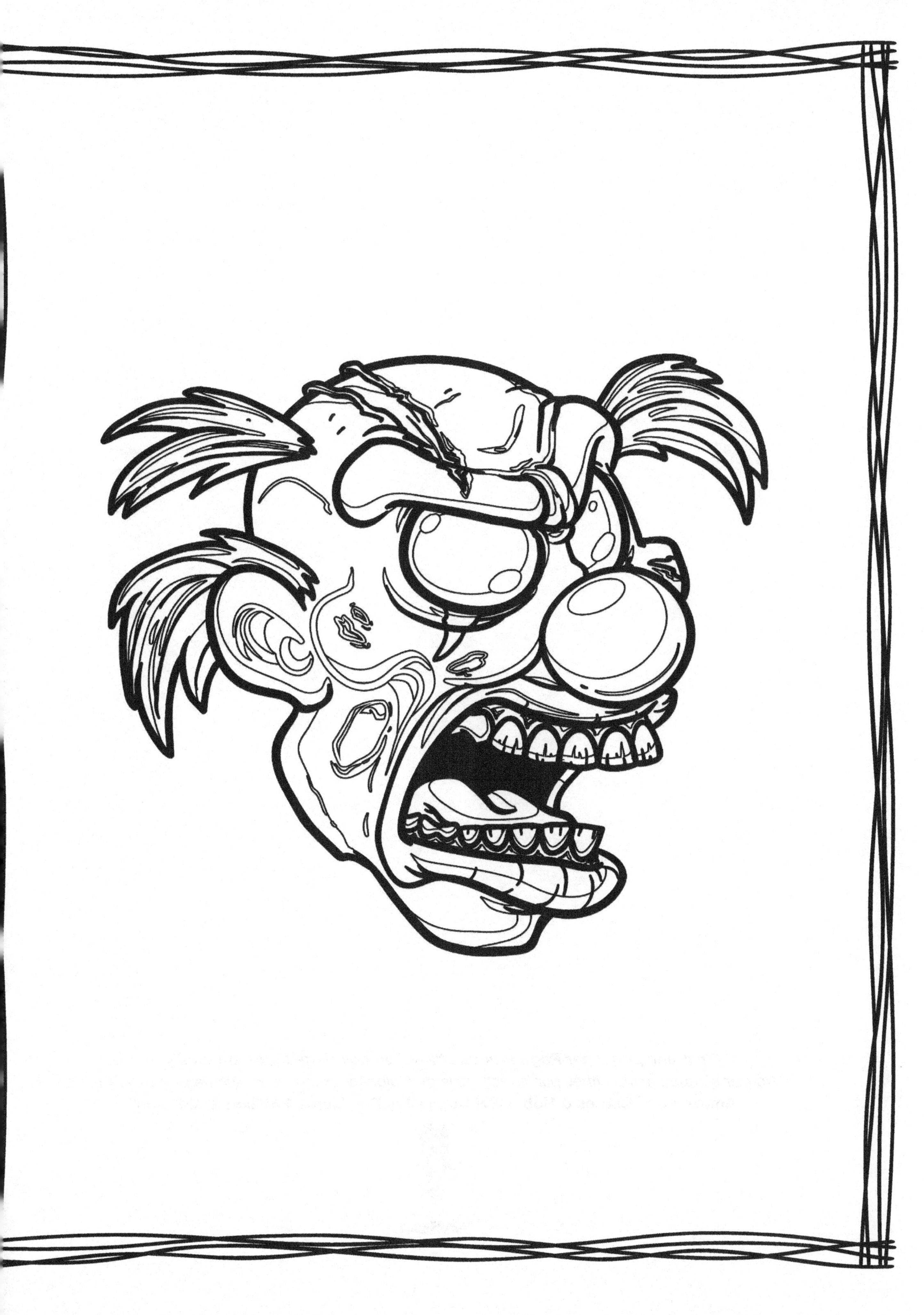

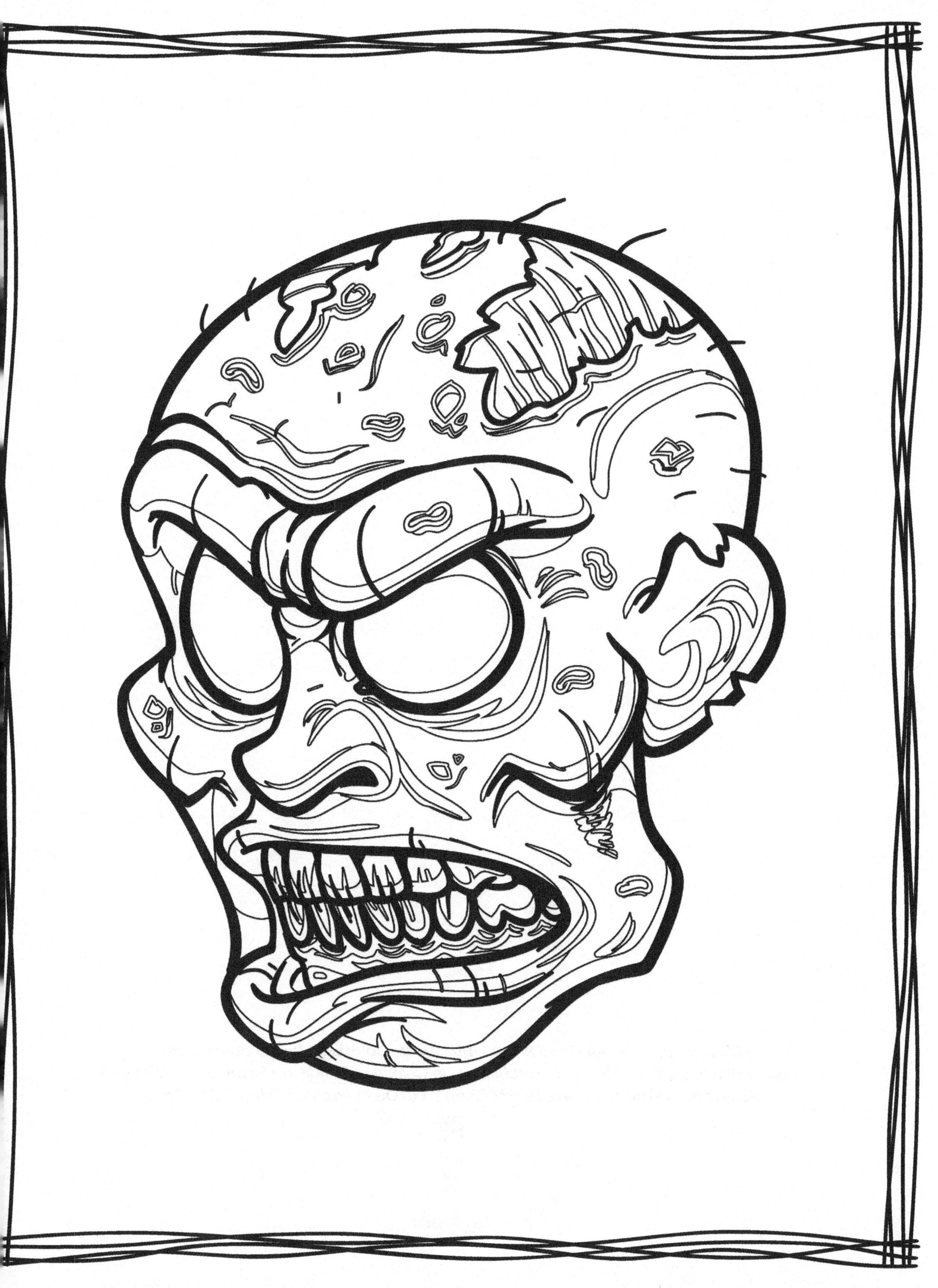

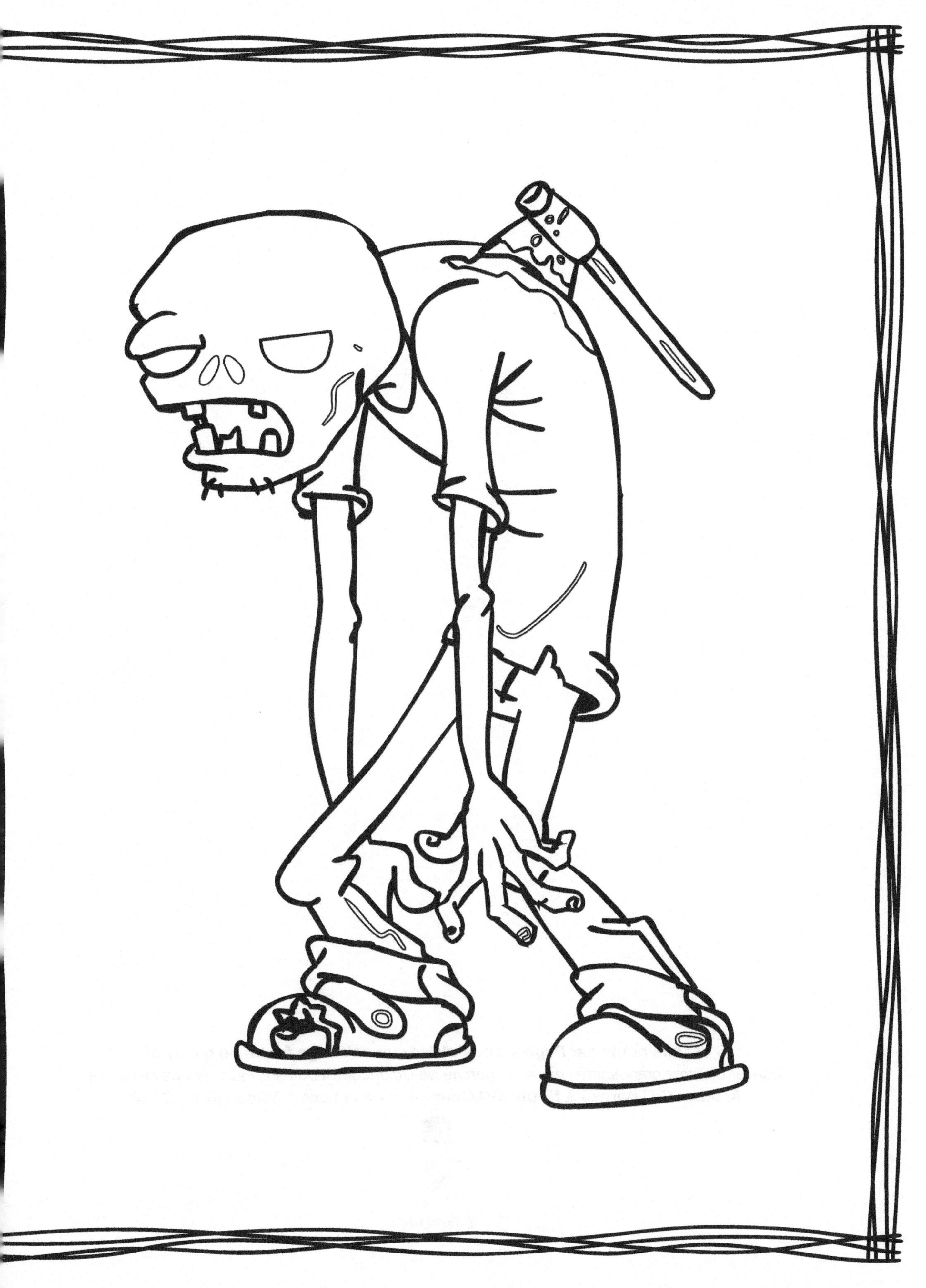

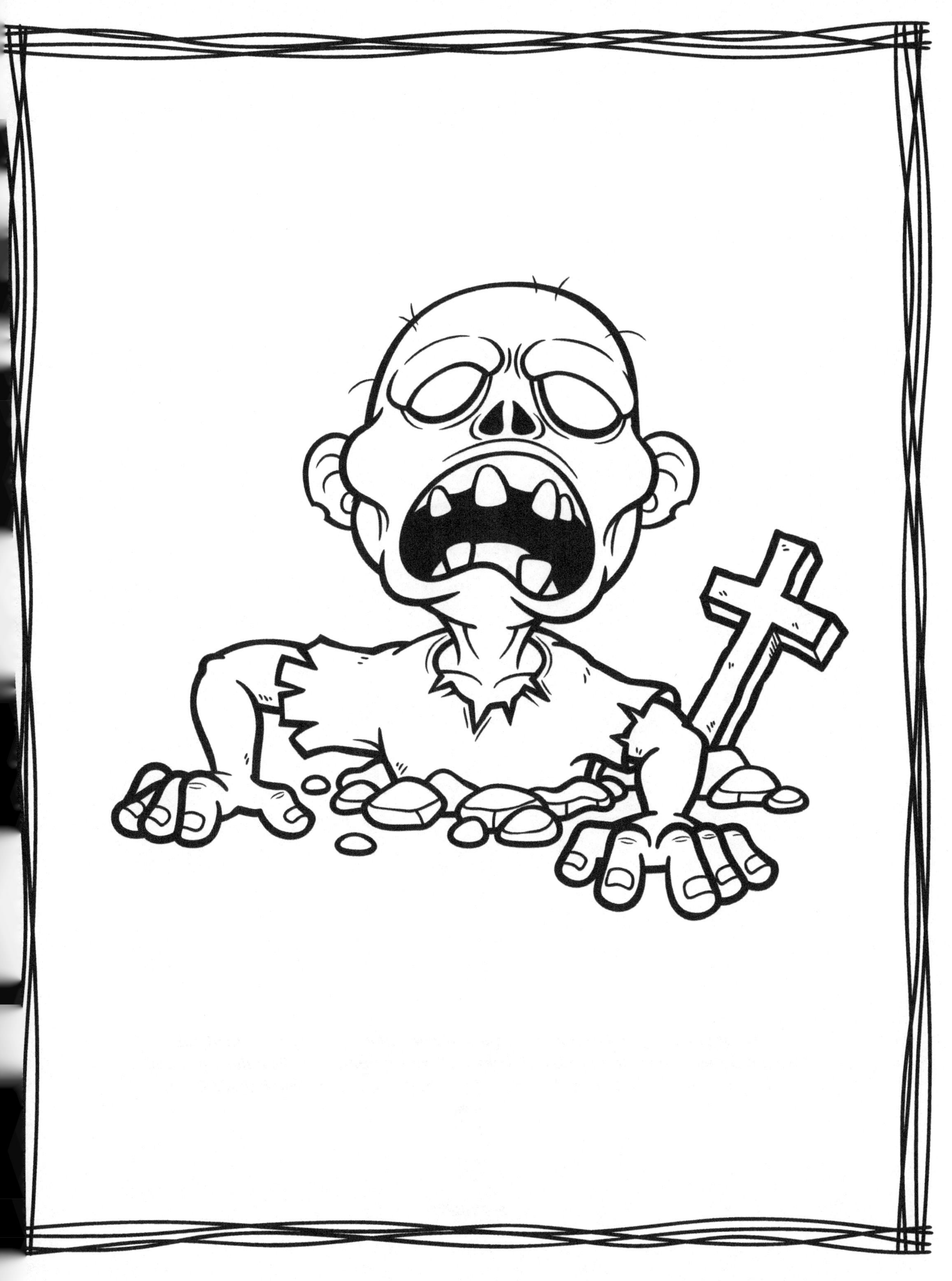

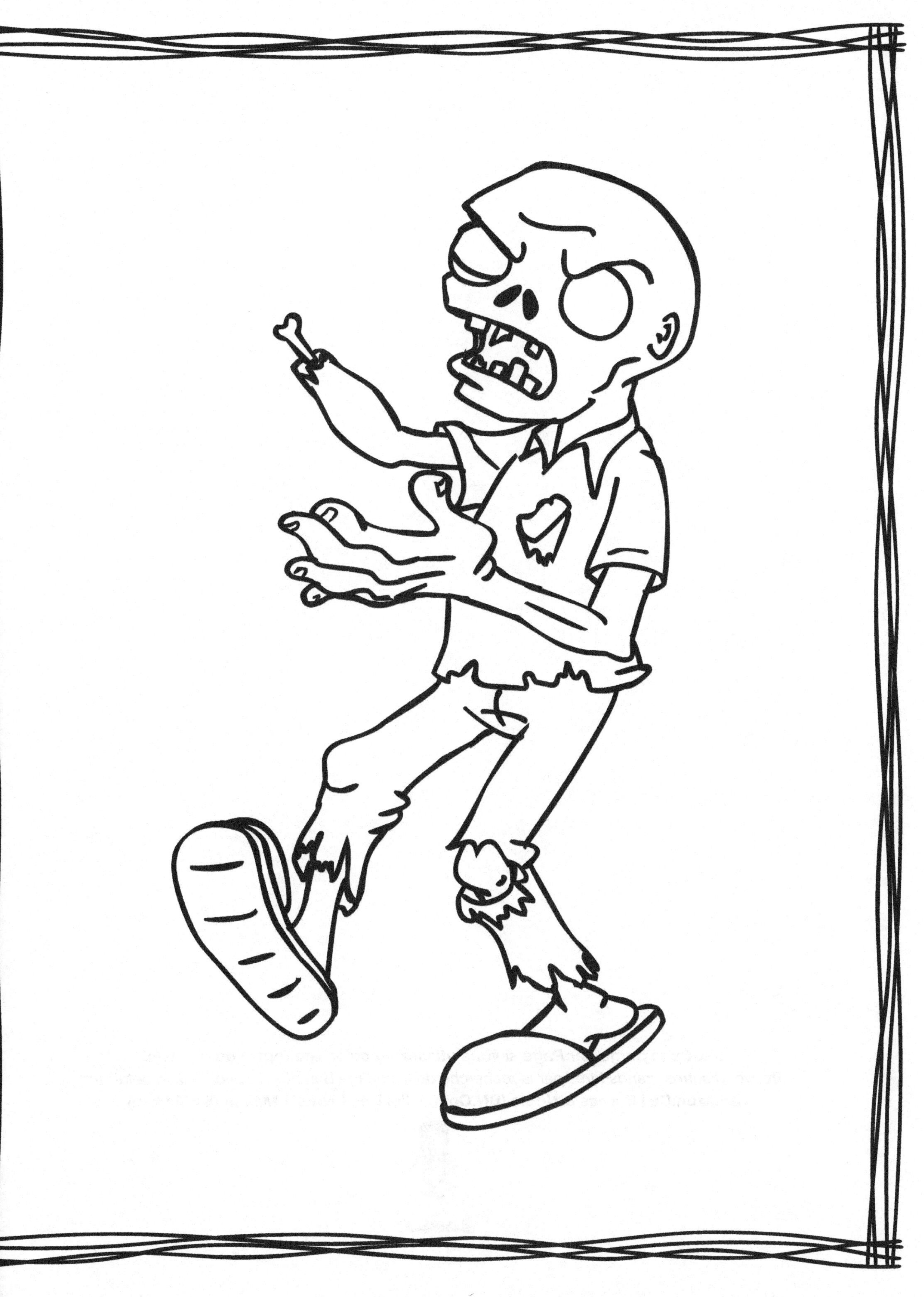

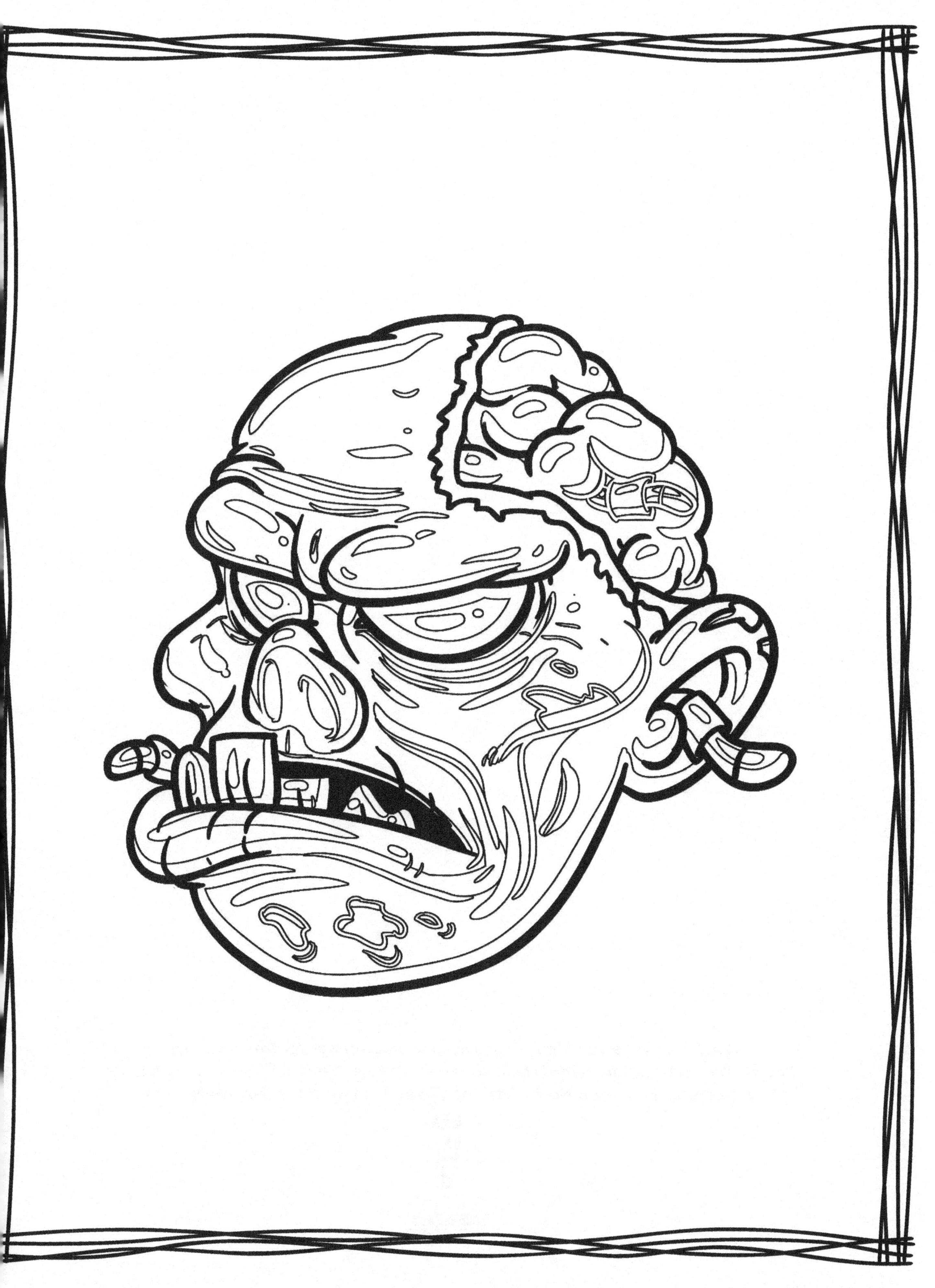

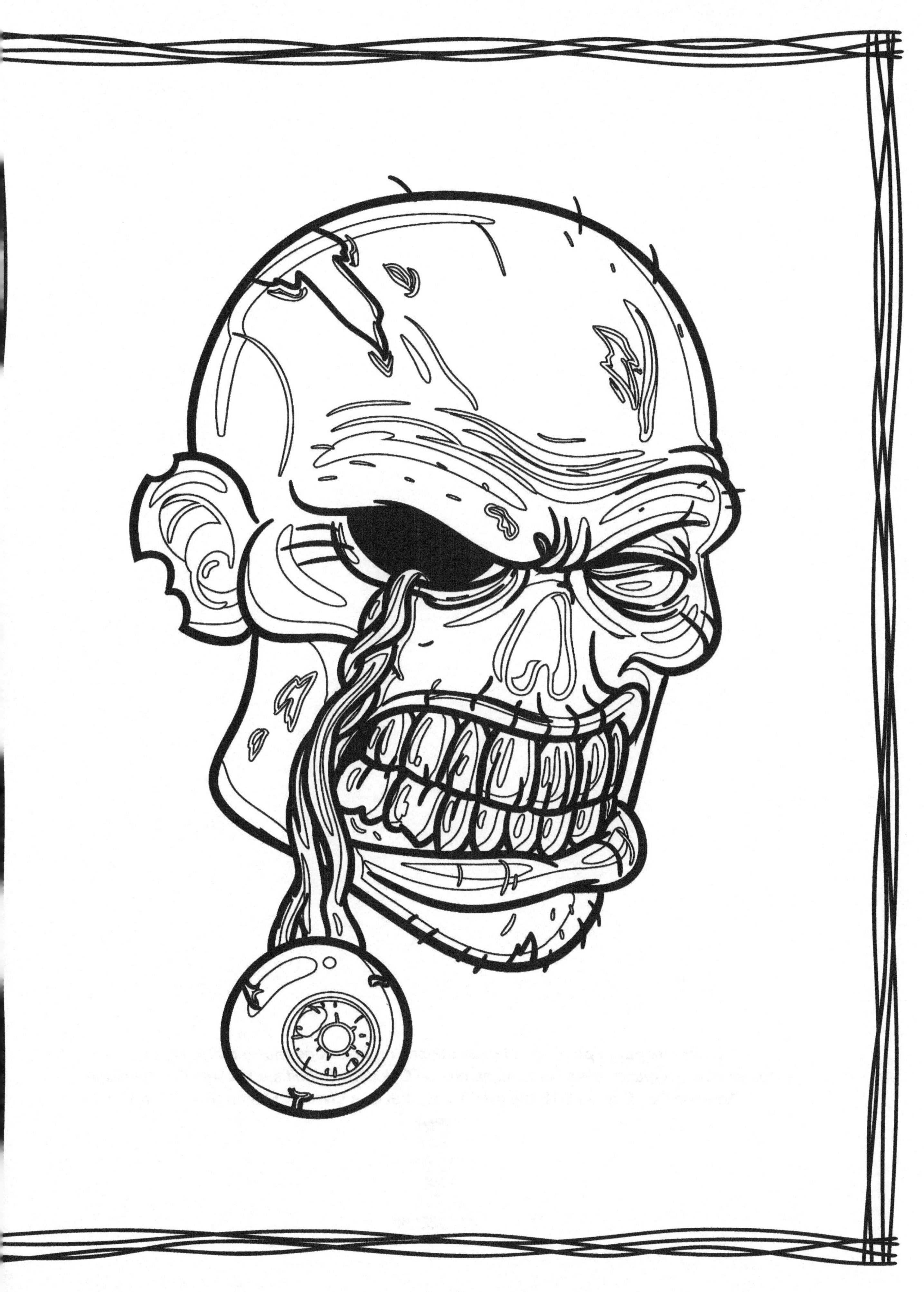

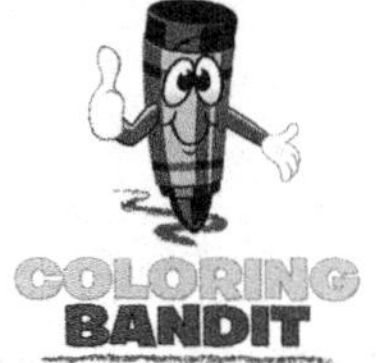

COLORING
BANDIT

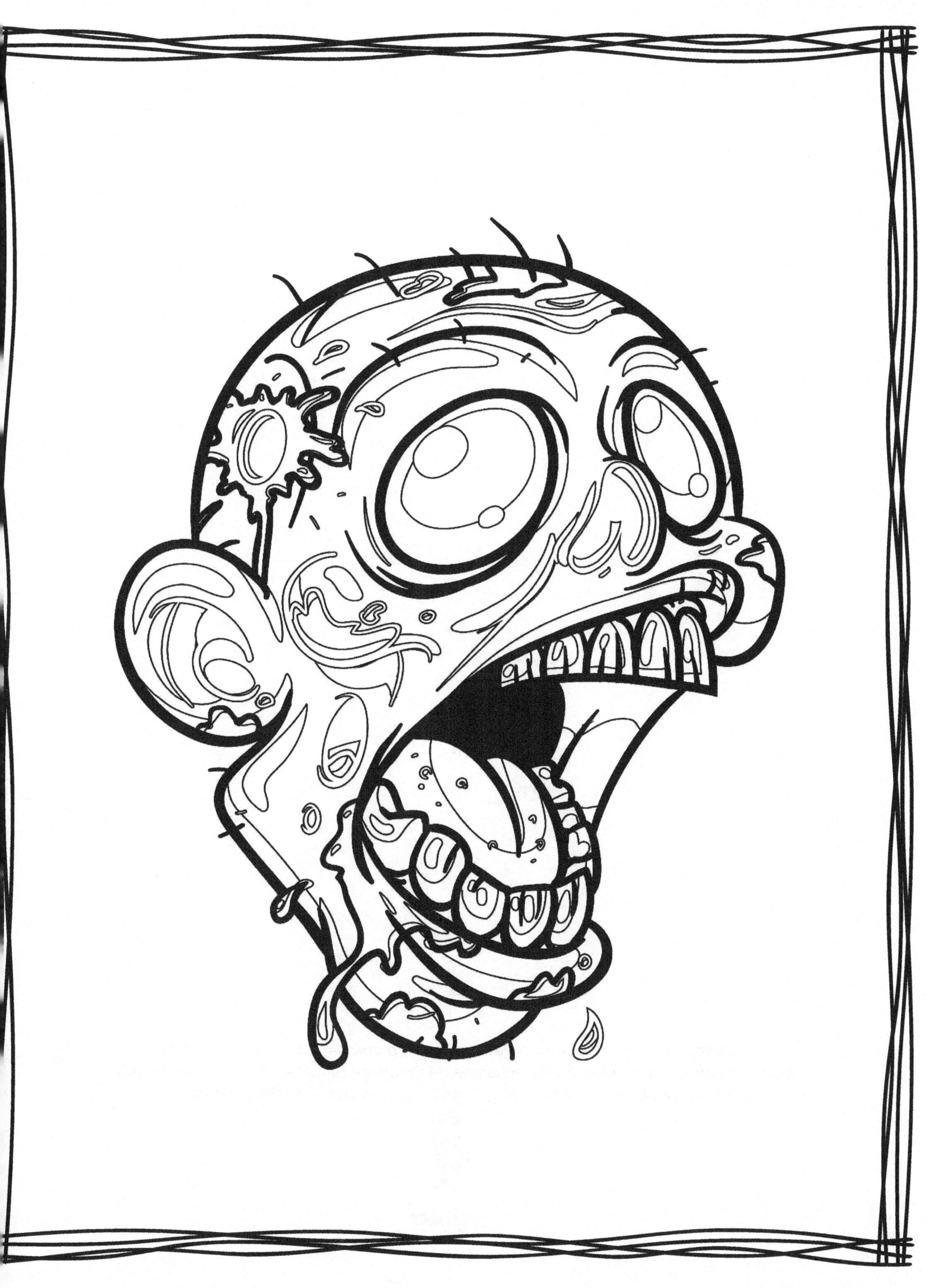

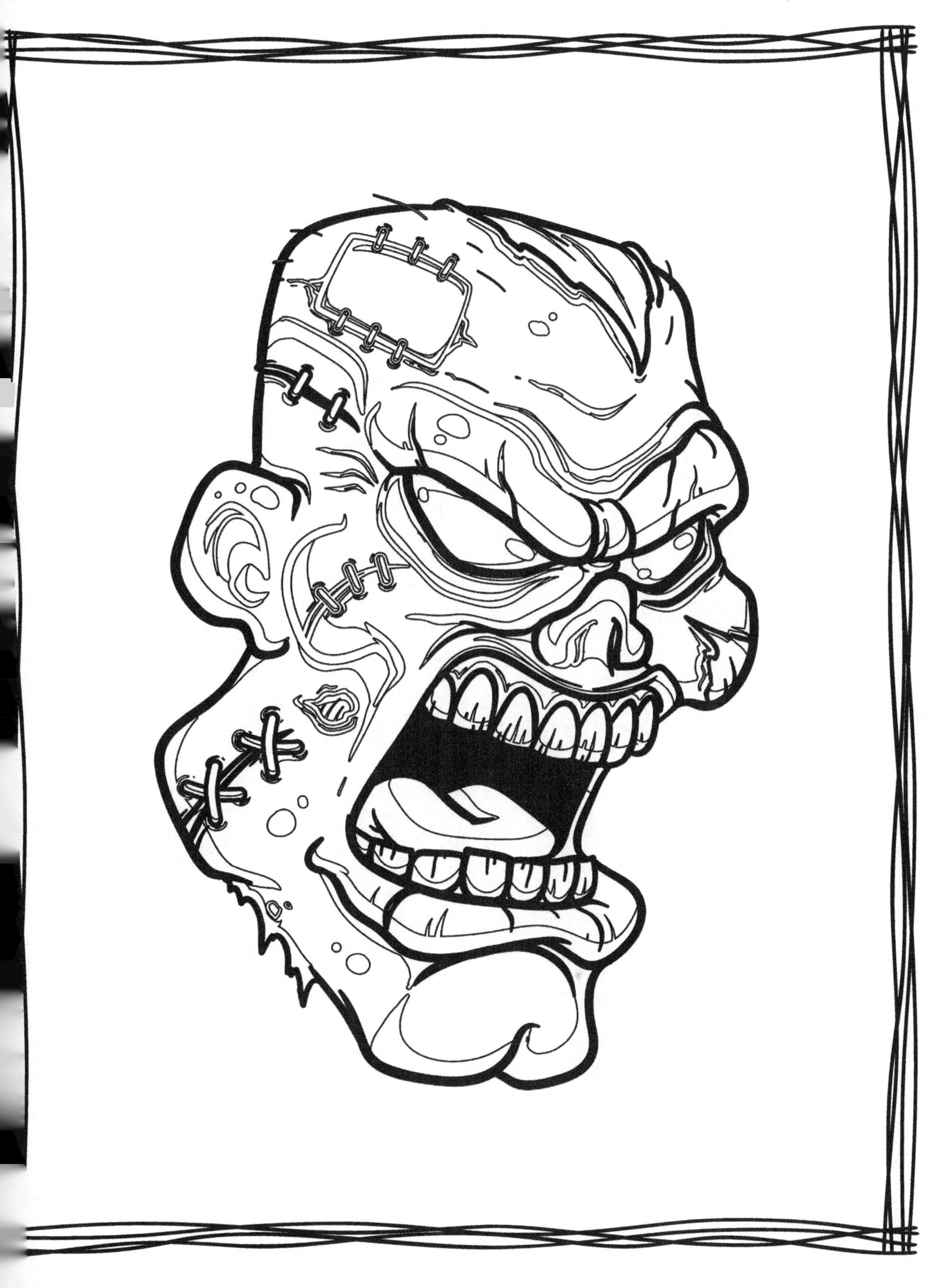

Made in the USA
Monee, IL
07 July 2026

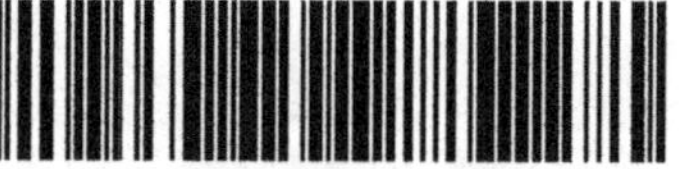

56547091R00037